My Blue Haven

ALSO BY ALEX DOULIS

Take Your Money and Run!

The Bond's Revenge

Tackling the Taxman

My Blue Haven

ALEX DOULIS

ECW PRESS

Published by ECW PRESS
2120 Queen Street East, Suite 200, Toronto, Ontario, Canada M4E 1E2

LIBRARY AND ARCHIVES CANADA CATALOGUING IN PUBLICATION

Doulis, Alex
My blue haven / Alex Doulis. — Rev. ed.

ISBN-13: 978-1-55022-772-7
ISBN-10: 1-55022-772-6

1. Tax havens. 2. Tax planning—Canada—Popular works.
I. Title.

HG179.D67 2007   343.7105'23   C2006-906817-8

Cover and text design: Tania Craan
Production: Mary Bowness
Printing: Transcontinental

This book is set in AGaramond

With the publication of *My Blue Haven* ECW PRESS acknowledges the generous financial
support of the Government of Canada through the Book Publishing Industry
Development Program (BPIDP) for our publishing activities. **Canadä**

DISTRIBUTION

CANADA: Jaguar Book Group, 100 Armstrong Ave., Georgetown, ON L7G 5S4

PRINTED AND BOUND IN CANADA

ECW PRESS
ecwpress.com

CONTENTS

Dedicated to:

Those who believe there can be no
financial security without confidentiality.

ACKNOWLEDGEMENTS

There are two groups to whom I am indebted for the motivation to write this book. The first are the many people who came out to hear me speak about my first book, *Take Your Money and Run!*, and complained that they were not yet ready to make a run for it but still wanted protection for their futures. These people were ordinary citizens who could see that much of what they had paid for with their tax dollars was not going to be available and that they would have to make their own preparations for their old age and failing health. They needed a few more years toiling in their respective vineyards before having the freedom to run. I hope that this book will tell them how to protect themselves.

It will seem unfair to many readers to single out just one other recipient to thank for the inspiration to write this book. Many will say that their own government is more profligate in its spending and avaricious in its tax policies than the Canadian government. However, I challenge all of you to find in your countries similar legislation enshrining the cronyism, sexism, and racism for which the Canadian taxpayer's dollars are used. Therefore, it is the Canadian government that can best be said to be the inspiration for this work.

Of course, some readers will argue that the rate at which promises of pensions, health care, and education are being refuted or eroded is faster in their countries than in Canada and that this would qualify their government as the most deserving recipient of my gratitude. That question cannot be answered without statistics. Where has the wait for a knee replacement increased the most? Which government has increased the pension age?

Thanks to all the men and women in Parliament and their handmaidens the bureaucrats, for their unflinching efforts to insure that the care and protection I was promised in my old age will be available only in half measures. Without their efforts, I would never have had to write this book or had such joy in doing so.

I am a mathematician and financial analyst. I am neither a lawyer nor an accountant. Therefore, I am not dispensing accounting or legal advice. However, at an early age I was required to learn to read. This led me to an understanding of the injustices of this world and in particular a tax system based on redistributing the wealth of the productive but not of the privileged. That same ability to read helped me understand the tax codes of Canada and the United States of America. They are really quite simple. They are formidable only because of their mass. I am inclined to believe that they are kept in their present form so that they will appear impenetrable by the layman. It is an old ploy and was used by stock-market bandits in the 1920s. When the markets' administrators asked that, to stop abuses, more disclosure be provided with new issues, the issuers of securities produced documents that looked like the Manhattan phonebook. This was just as good as providing no information as the task of finding the pertinent information buried in those tomes became formidable.

The tax systems in North America have functioned because people believe in their fairness. We have a self-assessing and voluntary payment system. When the fairness of the tax system begins to fall into doubt, then the ability to extract taxes becomes more difficult. In recent years, we have seen our tax money thrown around with reckless abandon. Don't fret about the one-time shots like the $40 screwdrivers for the U.S. Defense Department or the unused multimillion-dollar airport at Mirabel, Quebec. Concentrate more on the ongoing wealth distribution programs, such as the peanut subsidy. This program, which is costing hundreds of millions of dollars, made one man so wealthy that he could afford to run for the presidency of the United States, win the election, and spend the remainder of his time as a self-appointed diplomat. Is it any wonder that while in political office Jimmy Carter advocated an increase in the number and size of welfare programs? He was one of the great beneficiaries.

According to the early Greeks and the current crop of political scientists, the objective of government is to uphold the citizens' rights as outlined in their constitutions. At first, many governments decided how they were going to insure the citizens' rights. From there, the governments made decisions to provide outright benefits for some at a cost to others. In the Province of Ontario, the government would collect taxes from white males and then deny them the opportunity to seek jobs in the civil service. Yes, your thoughts are correct; that, pure and simply, is racism.

There is a clear government bias. Of the citizens of the Province of Ontario, blacks make up a clear colour-based minority. This minority has some alarming statistics — they have a higher suicide and victimization from violence rates and lower longevity and university entry rates. In light of these facts, how would you feel if the government gave funding to the majority white population to increase its already wealthier status rather than to the minority that is falling behind? You would be aghast. In the Province of Ontario, men, like blacks, are a minority and have the same appalling statistics described above. The response of the government to the plight of this gender-based minority was to give $8 million to groups dedicated to helping the majority — in other words, women's groups. Can you imagine the howls of protest if the government came up with a multimillion-dollar program to promote the betterment of white people, who, when compared to blacks, have the better profile? To me, it seems inconceivable that any government would treat one sex or one race better than the other or provide funds to groups who are benefitting as a result of being a majority of the population. Once you move from aiding minorities to aiding majorities, you are into some sort of "ism." But then, those are your racist, sexist tax dollars at work.

The realization by taxpayers that they are being fleeced has led to many forms of rebellion, the most common being pure and simple tax evasion, a legislated and punishable crime. Many of us would prefer to rebel in a legal way, as I have managed to do for many years now. My first rebellious act was in 1970. I had returned to Canada in 1969 to find that my tax load, in moving from the U.S., had increased by 50 percent. I then decided to be uncooperative with the tax department. After carefully reading the *Income Tax Act* to determine what constituted filing, I would staple all of my receipts to the tax form, leaving the rest of it blank and I would sign it and send it in without postage.

For four years, this was ignored by the tax department, but then they decided to put an end to my childish tantrum. They threatened me with an audit. This is usually an effective threat because most taxpayers have, to some extent, misrepresented their income either consciously or unconsciously and fear exposure. I replied that they had always done my tax preparation and that I would welcome an audit to determine their accuracy. They then threatened me with general prosecution. I replied that I had read the act and knew that they had no grounds, but that if they wanted to proceed I would insure full news coverage of the event to show other taxpayers a way to protest the tax system. Once they discovered that I knew the pertinent section of the law and the possible disruption I might cause their system, they capitulated; however, they did practise their own childish tantrum. I was probably the last person in the country to receive his annual refund.

More damaging than the occasional tax protest has been the advent of serious tax avoidance, which has led to the flight of investment capital from North America. The result, in just two of the tax havens, was that in 1994, 2,400 Canadians opened tax avoidance structures in the Cayman Islands and 28,000 Americans did so in the British Virgin Islands. This has led to the Cayman Islands having over $600 billion under administration, thus making it the third largest financial centre in the world. In Canada this has lead to the hiring of 'Avoidance Officers' by Canada Revenue Agency to investigate Canadians pursuing tax avoidance. You know things like RRSP contributions, flow through shares, and other avenues. Huh? I can hear you say, 'isn't tax avoidance legal?' Sure it is, but tax avoidance costs CRA money, so let's investigate and really scare the suckers.

Accompanying the flight of capital has been the flight of the owners of that capital. By flight I mean flying. Take the Rolling Stones. They rehearse in Canada, perform live in South America and record in Europe. All that flying occasioned by arcane income tax laws. Or you could look at Frank Stronach founder of Magna car parts manufacturing. Started the business in Canada but for tax purposes lives somewhere else.

We are at a dangerous crossroads where the number of people on the take is overtaking and outnumbering the number of people paying the bills. For example, there are 30 million people living in Canada, and the number of salary earners is less than 14 million. If you haven't read the Income Tax Act, either read it now or let me take you through the juicy bits. If you have any intention of providing a comfortable and healthy old age for yourself or for preserving your acquired wealth for future generations, then it is time for you to meet Stewart, who is about to learn full-body-contact, industrial-strength tax avoidance.

CHAPTER 1

How Do I Pay Thee?
LET ME COUNT THE WAYS

•••

At 6:00 p.m., on the first work day of the new year, I went down the elevator from my office in a skyscraper to have a drink with my colleagues before taking the 45-minute drive home. Usually, after the Christmas and New Year's holidays, people are feeling a little down, and since I am our office's "Mr. Brightside," I thought I might dispel the usual post-celebration gloom.

Ours is a small merchant banking and stock-trading organization with 13 partners and a high profitability. There is nothing like money to try to buy happiness. You can imagine my surprise when I arrived at our usual corner of the bar to find nothing but long faces and a rather animated debate taking place. I ordered a light beer and asked about the discourse. Had we missed a big trade? Lost out on a good piece of business?

"What's going on?" I asked Brian, the stock trader.

"You know how Avnar likes to stir the pot. Well, today he pointed out to us that we will be working until early June for the government before we start making any money for ourselves."

"What the hell is this all about?"

"Avnar maintains that by the time we have paid off our tax bill it is July. Then we start earning for ourselves."

"That's crazy," I said. "July is the start of the second half of the year. What he is saying is that we work half the year for the government. Avnar, you're nuts. We don't work half the year just to pay taxes. If that were true, we'd be paying 50 percent of our income in taxes."

At this point, our economist piped up. "I am afraid, dear boy, he is right."

"Charles, I read just the other day that the government's average income tax rate in Canada is around 35 percent of income. So, how do you two come up with a 50 percent tax rate?"

Avnar said, "Because 'Tax Freedom' day in Canada is June fifth."

"Avnar," I said, "that is a circular argument."

"What Avnar is saying is true in one respect," replied Charles. "The real total rate of taxation in Canada is 40 percent down from 48 in recent years."

"Whose number is that?" I asked.

"The Fraser Institute."

"Those guys have their numbers all mixed up," I said.

"I read in a government publication that on average

they take just over 35 percent, not 40 percent, of earned income. Also, the rate could not have gone from 48 percent to 40 percent because I haven't seen anything like a 8 percent tax cut announced."

"But that doesn't include the hidden taxes, and you have received a 5 percent deferred tax reduction," replied Charles.

Now I have always considered myself a bit of a forensic accountant and I have seen deferred taxes but only in corporate accounts. I have never seen, while dissecting government statements, an item labeled "deferred taxes." I was starting to get a little hot under the collar with Charles's naivety.

"I wish they would teach you economists a little accounting in those ivory towers where you are educated. I have read the statements in the budget for the past dozen years and never seen an item labeled 'deferred taxes' in the government's accounts. There is no such thing."

"Cool down, Stewart," said Charles. "It is a question of terminology. When the government uses all its tax collected funds to pay for gun registries and graft to Quebec advertising firms and finds the coffers empty it borrows money from the world to pay for other important things like holidays for the anointed and the entitlements of the entitled. Instead of you paying the tax bite needed for the spending it will be left to future generations when the borrowings are redeemed. In recent years the government has not run to the bond markets to borrow because it has been running fiscal surpluses. The Goods and Services Tax (GST) they campaigned to remove has been a gold mine for them. So the amount of deferred tax is being reduced instead of increased. The government is actually running a surplus."

"Yeah," Brian, the stock trader said, "so much so that they've given the corporations a tax break."

A voice from somewhere said, "Corporations don't pay taxes. Their customers pay their taxes."

"Hold it just a minute," Brian, the stock trader, said. "I've seen in the papers that companies are paying millions in taxes. So you can't say they don't pay taxes."

"What you are missing, Brian, is that the taxes are actually paid by the person buying the corporation's product or services. When the mechanic works on that fancy car of yours, he charges you $65 per hour. He only wants to make $45 per hour but has to charge you an extra $20 to pay his taxes. So you are paying his taxes and everybody else's taxes who you do business with."

"That is still historical, or should I say hysterical," I replied. "This latest government was elected on a platform that included fiscal restraint, which should maintain balanced budgets."

"Really? You believe that fiscal restraint fairy tale? This government is in the black not because of lower expenditures. The expenditures in the year 2000 were up 6.6 percent and the debt charges were up 1.3 percent over 1999. It is only because government revenues were up by 10.1 percent that there is a surplus and even that is less than 3 percent of the official debt. If you want a clear picture of what is happening in this country look at after-tax incomes. That is the amount of money that you actually have to spend. In 1981 Canadians had 90 percent of the disposable income of our neighbours to the south. Today we have 65 percent of their disposable income. We're getting screwed. I'm going to make a prophecy. When the next recession really bites, the government will spend the surplus to support the economy."

"That's exactly what they should do according to Keynesian economics," I said.

"Certainly, Stewart, but the problem is that they increased spending during a boom period and you now expect the government to do the same in a bust. When do they decrease spending? It seems never. Therefore, don't expect any ongoing tax relief."

I sat back in my chair while the debate raged around me. I didn't need my workmates to explain it any further. The government was spending like crazy and would soon be putting the expense on its credit card. Being a financial analyst, my question was, "What did that mean for the future?"

Obviously if you get too deep in hock on your credit card, your bankers start to worry. A couple of years back, I saw in the papers that the bond-rating agencies were contemplating cutting the country's credit rating. As well, there were now questions being raised about the sanctity of the Canada Pension Plan. It seemed there was not going to be enough money or taxing power in the country to cover the obligations. Then it struck me that the nation was going to the pawn shop. The government was selling the industries that it owned in order to be able to keep spending.

With an air of despair, I said, "Well guys, be happy that the tax freedom day is in early June. From what Charles says, taxes won't be going down. If anything they'll increase."

"You know," said Charles, "I wish that accountants like you, Stewart, were given at least a bit of economic education in those training programs they force you to endure. Had they done so you might be aware of the Laffer curve."*

I could have made a pun about the name, but you never pushed Charles too far. He was the most sensitive economist I had ever met. In fact, you never called him Charlie, so I responded in the approved manner. "Gosh, Charles, what pray tell is the Laffer curve?"

"Charles Laffer was an American economist who discovered that there are two rates of income tax that produce roughly the same revenue to the government. They each fall on either side of 50 percent. For example, the U.S. government had a tax rate of 7 percent in 1916 on incomes over $300,000, which produced about $80 million in rev-

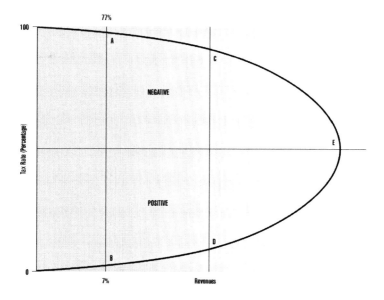

*The graph shows that at points A and B the revenues achieved by the U.S. government were the same although the tax rates differed by 70 percent. As tax rates rose from 0 to 50 percent, tax revenues increased and then began to decrease approaching zero at a 100 percent tax rate.

enue. In 1921, it increased the rate to 77 percent and raised $85 million. At 7 percent there were 1,296 returns filed and in 1921 only 246."

"So they had a recession or something," I said.

"Not so, old boy. They had tax evasion and avoidance as you can see from the decrease in the number of tax filers."

Then someone at the table said, "Demographics, that'll take care of deficit."

"I wouldn't count on that," said Charles. "Demographics are actually working against us. For example, you take the government pension plan. Running a pension fund is not a rocket-scientist endeavour. It works like this. You collect from all the future beneficiaries a constant stream of payments until they reach retirement age. You take the money you collect and invest it in the country's economy and then pay them out from the growth in the earnings and value of the investments. You don't need to do any better than the growth in the value of the Dow Jones average to provide everybody with a decent retirement. In fact, you will probably have more money left than you promised to pay out. So, can you expect a pretty nice little sum from the social security you paid in the U.S. or the Canada Pension Plan or Old Age Supplement in Canada? That's the way it's supposed to work and it does if you play by the rules, but the people who ran our pension funds have not been playing by the rules.

"If the three funds mentioned above continue to pay out at current rates they will be out of money ten years after the turn of the millennium because those plans were never properly funded. They were based on the thesis that there would always be more new workers coming into the system than were retiring, and hence an ever increasing stream of payments to finance the retired workers. If I set up a plan like that, it would be called a Ponzi scheme* and I would be telling you this from jail. To illustrate, let's take the government's pension scheme to its ultimate end. What happens when North America is shoulder to shoulder with people and there is no room for the incremental workers we are counting on to pay the future pensions? Obviously, we cannot have any more new workers and the promises have to be revoked.

"So how did we arrive at this mess? At first it looked pretty good. In 1940, there were 40 workers per retiree. That fell to 17 in 1950, four in 1990, and will fall to two by the year 2020. What has happened is that the birth rate in North America has declined dramatically. In 1986, the fertility of North American women (which is the number of children each woman could be expected to bear in her life) was 1.8. In 1900, the rate was almost four times as high, and even in the early 1970s, there were 2.3 births per woman. With 1.8 births per woman, we are not even replacing ourselves. What has happened to the birth rate?

"It has long been an axiom, in our economist fraternity, that the best method of birth control is industrialization. This occurs because in agrarian societies, as North America was at the turn of the century, children are an asset in the form of more hands to work the fields. Children also form the basis of a pension because they work the fields of their parents until death passes the land on to the willing hands

---

* Ponzi schemes were originated by Charles Ponzi who in Boston in the late 1800s paid his investors outrageously high rates of interest from the capital he received from new investors. Eventually he ran out of new investors and the scheme collapsed.

of the children. In industrialized societies, there is no financial benefit from siring children except when state benefits are based on the number of children. No matter how many children assembly-line workers produce, the standard of living of the assembly-line workers will not increase and they can have little hope that their children will stay at home to provide for them in their old age. In fact, assembly-line workers, doctors, and bankers can only see their standard of living diminish by producing children, as children no longer increase their parents' productive capacity but become an expense item. Thus, in nations where production comes from the soil, we see birth rates that are higher than the birth rates in nations where wealth comes from goods that are produced or from specialized services that are rendered. So where does that leave us?

"It produces some interesting numbers. For instance, roughly 20 percent of the baby boom generation will have no children. Who is going to pay their pensions? In the year 2016, 16 percent of Canada's population will be over 65 years old while the number of under 18-year-olds will have fallen from 25 percent to 20 percent.

"So far, I have only spoken of half the problem, that being the falling birth rate in North America. It gets worse. People are living longer. Prior to the 1960s less than 10 percent of the population could be expected to live beyond 65. Today 80 percent of North Americans can be expected to live beyond 65. According to a Rand Corporation study, the life expectancy of a baby born in North America in the year 2000 will be 90 years. The tremendous advances in medical technology, such as the MRI and CAT scan equipment, combined with strides in pharmacology, have dramatically increased longevity.

"This has drastically altered the age profile of the U.S. as well. In July 1983, the number of people over 65 exceeded teenagers for the first time in the country's history. By the year 2025, it is likely that seniors will outnumber teenagers in North America by a ratio of 2:1. I'll bet that you now understand some of the recent government policies. Immigration, they hope, will get us off the hook. If we can bring in enough of those under 30-year-olds, they will pay the medical and pension bills for all those who were promised benefits. There is a slight problem. Some of those immigrants come from countries where the taxes are extracted to keep the power holders (local dictators or warlords, as the case may be) in the style to which they have become accustomed. It is therefore culturally acceptable for them to deny the tax man every cent possible. Those cultures, along with other differences, are imported to North America.

"Now let me see if I've got this right. We are going to ask all those people we suckered into coming here to pay the unfunded pension liabilities we acquired in the past, so we native-born Canadians could have a Florida vacation every winter. Look around you and notice that General Motors, Ford, and many other companies have been bankrupted by their pension and health plans. Companies around the world are reducing or closing their plans to new workers. What you are seeing is the nation's problems in a microcosm."

At this point, Brian, the stock trader who was always looking at the benign side of human character, said, "Actually, Charles, most people in a democracy do accept their civic responsibilities, even if corporations don't."

"It's not a case of wanting to do the right thing, it's a matter of capability. Okay, let's say you are a dyed-in-the-wool liberal. You believe that every person has a conscience and they will do the right thing irrespective of culture, race, age, et cetera. The Organization for Economic Cooperation and Development estimates that tax rates would have to go to 65 percent just to support the present level of pension and health care benefits promised to the baby boomers. Now that doesn't allow anything for current expenditures on education, health, and welfare. So, the next generation and all those immigrants who left oppressive societies are going to be oppressed into paying a 65 percent tax rate and get nothing back. That, obviously, is not the answer to the dilemma.

"Let me emphasize, gentlemen, I am not describing events that might happen. These are demographic events already set in place. The fact that conservative governments are being elected reflecting the thoughts of 55-year-olds rather than 25-year-olds should be enough of an indicator of whom is the major age group. What I've told you is that they are just the advance party. Let me put it more succinctly. The die is cast, the gun is loaded, and the dice are coming up snake eyes for your pension."

"Wait," said a voice in the corner, "the government can do as it has always done and that is borrow the money until this problem subsides. It's sort of like borrowing to wage war."

"Let's look at government borrowing," retorted the economist. "Originally governments borrowed for specific capital purposes, such as a road, dam, or building. They then pledged that asset as collateral against that loan, which is

why government debts are usually referred to as bonds*
rather than as debentures. These bonds would then be
retired by a tax on the users of the facility or in some cases,
such as bridges and roads, a toll. However, current practice
would dictate that government bonds should in most cases
be called debentures. Debentures are securities obligating a
borrower to pay without the backing of a specific asset as
collateral. North American governments acquired some of
their nastier financial habits as a result of wars during which
they began borrowing for 'General Coffers' by issuing
debentures and taxing incomes. This nastiness was justified
by the necessity to win against the morally corrupt enemy,
after which, the nastiness would be done away with in a
manner as swift as the handling of war criminals. Regret-
tably, the tax, which American legislators felt so unfair and
heinous during the American Civil War and Canadians
adopted as a temporary measure in the First World War, was
found to be so lucrative and empowering for the politicians
that it could not be revoked. After all, money is power, and
if you have the electorate's money, you have their power.
Politicians pursue their vocation as a result of the lust for
power. Why give that back to the masses?

"Power is a narcotic. The politicians had to have more
each decade and so income taxes went up relentlessly. But,
after a 40 percent tax rate, the amount of money raised no
longer increased, and as rates went even higher, both economic activity and total tax take decreased. Your elected

---

* Bonds are securities issued witnessing a loan backed by an asset. These are
essentially mortgages. Debentures resemble a line of credit in that they are
unbacked by any asset but are an obligation by the corporation to pay
interest and principal when due.

representatives did not want to seem powerless to supply even more and better programs, so they resorted to debt to pay for them. After all, you are not going to deny the wife and kiddies a trip to Disneyland this winter, so if you have no cash in your pocket, you'll just put it on the credit card. Dad maintains his image of the great provider even though he can't pay for it. For the politicians, the debt was never a problem because when it came time to pay the piper they knew that they would probably not be in office. Look at what your elected representative has done: he has deferred the taxes necessary to provide you benefits until he is out of office. The reality is somebody in the future is going to have to pay that debt and it may or may not be done with income taxes."

"As our resident economist, Charles, would you care to tell us what to expect rather than increased income taxes?" I asked.

"Obviously, there has to be some sort of wealth tax. Assets such as houses, pension savings, and investment capital will be taxed. It has already been talked about and the trial balloons have been run up in the press. Leaked rumours before the 1995 Canadian government budget spoke of imposing a tax on pension savings over $500,000. Recently the U.S. government planners discussed a one-time 15 percent tax on all private U.S. pension assets to top up social security. If not now, why not in the future? Why do you think the Bronfmans took their billions out of the country, not to mention the Irvings, Stronachs, and on and on?

"The reason I spent my Christmas holidays with statistics on government spending and demographics while you all were into your cups is because this will all have an impact on currencies. The early 1990s saw a round of competitive devaluations of currencies on a worldwide basis. Because everyone was doing it, neither inflation nor competitive advantage changed dramatically for the participants. However, in the future, the depreciation of a country's currency may be externally imposed rather than a policy choice of its government. Take, for example, Canada's position: 40 percent of the country's debt is in the hands of foreigners. When they bought those bonds from the Canadian government, the foreign investors had to go into the currency markets and buy Canadian dollars in order to pay for them. This had the effect of pushing up the price of the Canadian dollar in the early 1970s when Canada first went on a borrowing binge. When those investors redeem their bonds, they will be paid in Canadian dollars, which they will immediately sell for yen, marks, or pounds. This will have the effect of depressing the value of the Canadian dollar."

"You're all wet, Charles," said the stock trader. "The dollar hit near-term highs in 2005. It's going higher."

"The dollar is doing well with respect to the U.S. dollar. But what about other foreign currencies? The rate with respect to those is virtually unchanged. What you are witnessing is the falling U.S. dollar — not a climbing Canadian dollar. And how long do you think the Canadian government will allow Quebec paper plants and furniture factories to continue to close while Alberta continues to hand out money to its residents? We do 85 percent of our trade with the U.S.A. and if their currency sinks because of their profligacy then ours will have to join it or see our country close down."

"How can they bring down our dollar?" I asked.

"The classical way is to inflate the currency. I use the term 'classical' in its truest sense. This is a time-proven device to overcome government financial problems. As far back as 421 BC, it was being bemoaned by writers. Aristophanes, in the play *The Wasps*, had the following stanza:

Where is the silver drachma of old?
Or the recent gold coins,
So clean stamped and worth their weight,
Through the known world have ceased to circulate,
Now days Athenian shoppers go to market,
With their pockets full of shoddy, silver plated coppers.

"We are currently overtaxed because our government is running a surplus. When will it end?" Avnar asked.

"Likely never. Governments don't want to reduce taxation because money is power. The ultimate power is communism with its 100 percent taxation. Governments will always tax to the limit of the Laffer curve one way or the other."

"What do you mean, 'one way or the other'?"

"Governments have always looked for new ways to tax. You see, in England at one time they tried to introduce a tax on people based on the number of fireplaces in their houses. After it was found by the courts that the tax inspectors had no right to enter a home to determine the number of hearths, the tax men went to a system based on the number of windows. The windows were boarded up and skylights invented. In fact, whole societies have collapsed because of taxation and bloody wars fought."

"Charles, you really do get carried away a little. Tell me of the last bloody war fought over taxation," I said.

"The American Civil War."

"You're crazy," I said. "That was fought over slavery."

"No, the self-aggrandizing in American society would have you believe that all those lives were lost at places like Gettysburg and Bull Run so that coloured people could walk free in the land. Not so. Slavery was not abolished until well after the war was underway. In fact, Lincoln had pretty well guaranteed the South that they would be able to continue but not expand slave operations. Think back to what was the event that touched off the war? Firing on Fort Sumter. Fort Sumter was a Union fort in Charleston Harbor where the hated federal tariffs were collected.

"The South's economy was based on exports while the North's strength was manufacturing. The South wanted to sell its cotton for cheap foreign imported goods rather than purchase expensive northern goods. To pay back his political supporters in the North, Lincoln passed the 'Morill Tariff' bill in 1857, which doubled the rates on imported goods. This bill effectively sucked the money out of the South for the benefit of the North. So, the South decided to secede from the Union.

"Stewart, can you imagine how banal it would sound if the masses knew that all those young men who died at Gettysburg did so over taxes?"

"Speaking of Gettysburg," I said, "didn't Lincoln's Gettysburg Address start with the statement, 'Four score and seven years ago our fathers brought forth on this continent a new nation conceived in liberty and dedicated to the proposition that all men are created equal.'?"

"Yes, but it ended with the statement, 'this nation under God shall have a new birth of freedom, and that government of the people, by the people, for the people shall not perish from the earth.' You can see where Lincoln's sentiment lay. He was more interested in preserving the government of the North, which he regarded as being for the people because it was beneficial to his industrialist supporters."

"Tell me, Charles, what makes you such an authority?" I asked.

"I read, dear boy. I would suggest, if you really want to bone up on taxes, which constitute a major portion of the accountant's day, that you start with Charles Adams's book *For Good and Evil*, which is a wonderful history of taxation. Drop over to my desk tomorrow and I'll lend you my copy."

One of my partners said that our salvation lay in buying politicians such as the Prime Ministers as they were fairly cheap and they brought great benefits. He was referring to one of our competitors having kept Jean Chrétien on their payroll as a 'Consultant' for $50,000 per year for which they were given a bounty of business by not just the Liberals but the Conservatives as well.

"Don't be silly," the economist said. "It's not what you make, it's what you keep and as the law stands in Canada you don't even own what you keep as there is no guarantee of property rights in our constitution."

As the discussion continued, I sat back and wondered which was more distressing. Losing a debate with Charles or hearing him say that I could never be rich. At least, if I had some idea of what to expect, I could plan accordingly. What were the government's options?

Reduce spending? Not likely. The last three Canadian and U.S. governments had been elected on platforms of debt reduction but the actualities were just the opposite. The U.S. government had narrowly defeated a balanced budget amendment to its constitution. Although the balanced budget was highly sought by the electorate, their representatives knew better and put that to rest. However, while I was contemplating this, I heard Avnar and Charles tossing around some thoughts on spending.

"I don't mind some taxes to support the poor," said Avnar. "But I do object to all the corporate handouts. The number of poor people is increasing and at the same time the corporations are withholding money from their tax payments to the government."

"Actually," the economist said, "the number of poor people is increasing because the poor are doing better. In the province of Ontario, which is not atypical, the number of people on welfare increased from 5 percent of the population in 1985 to 11 percent by 1995. This did not occur because there were more people in dire straits but because wages in the welfare field had gone up by between 18 and 43 percent, in real terms, over the period. If you want to induce people into a profession, then you increase the earnings in that profession. Therefore, with higher wages in the welfare drawing profession the number of participants increased."

"Welfare recipients don't get wages," somebody said.

"Call it what you want, people on welfare still receive money and the amount they took home monthly increased faster than wages in the private sector, which on average climbed by only 2.5 percent over the same period. This increase in salary levels of welfare recipients encouraged people to leave their low-paying jobs for the better-paying positions that they received from social assistance. The result of all this government largesse was that the bottom 10 percent of wage earners brought home 17 percent less than the average welfare earner. As an illustration of the wage sensitivity of welfare recipients, note that 19 percent of those in Ontario chose to accept other employment when the provincial government cut their take-home pay by 22 percent. More than 180,000 people collecting welfare decided that they preferred the higher wages in the private sector and left the dole.* Also, Avnar, don't be cute. You may only be a stock salesman but with an M.B.A. degree, I'm sure that you know that the so-called deferred tax item on a corporate balance sheet is only a bookkeeping entry showing the different rate at which equipment depreciates on a tax basis versus a utility basis. If you want to talk about handouts, why don't you mention your political friends? Wasn't that one of your drunken political hack buddies I just saw appointed to the senate? How much is that going to cost the taxpayers?"

"Charlie, ease up. It's only about a hundred grand a year, all in."

"Avnar, my name is Charles, and it's not just your buddy, there are about another 3,000 political appointments in this country at $100,000 a year. That's over a quarter of a billion dollars a year just for political payoffs, which is significant percent of the annual deficit. Then there is the pork barrelling. How about the Mirabel Airport or the $3.65 billion of government money that has gone to Bombardier over the past ten years? Therein lies one of the reasons for big government budgets — the budget has to be big to be able to hide all the slop."

"Enough," I said. "This isn't going anywhere. How can

---

* On February 28th, 2001, the *National Post* reported that jobs at a Newfoundland call centre could not be filled because of the attraction of higher benefits from unemployment.

you protect yourself? How can you stop the rip off? Give me something I can work with."

"From what I've heard, there is very little in the way of options," said Brian, the trader. "The southern States tried armed rebellion and that got them nowhere. The ballot box is a joke. It seems in most countries elected leaders spend their later years under investigation or in jail. With their code of ethics, I guess you can't expect them to keep their promises. Perhaps that is why they are called 'Honourable' in the House of Commons. It is sort of an inside joke. The only 'out' I can see is to take the route of our ex-partner Angelo and make a run for it. Although, since Angelo's book *Take Your Money and Run!* — which describes his escape from indentured service — was published, the government is making it even more difficult to shed your residency. The non-residency form, which was one page in Angelo's time, is now four pages long."

I remembered what Brian was describing. Our former partner Angelo had decided that at 50 years old he was running out of lifespan, but he couldn't see how to finance his existence without working. Then Angelo concluded that if he could eliminate his highest cost-of-living expense, income tax, from his life, he would double his income and double his fun. He determined that most countries tax on the basis of residency, and that if he wasn't a resident of Canada, he would be able to get out of the clutches of Canada Revenue Agency. He shed his Canadian residency status and became a resident of Ireland and lived happily ever after.

However, shedding one's tax residency is getting harder. I have done some research and found that the British Inland Revenue hangs on to you for another three years after you leave. You may have given up your British residency and moved to the Bahamas but for a period of three years, the U.K. will designate you as domiciled in Great Britain. This means that you are not entitled to any of the privileges of a resident, such as health and education, but you are required to pay tax on all payments originating in the U.K. Also, your estate will be probated in the U.K. with the appropriate inheritance tax extracted if you should pass away before three years.

The U.S. is even worse. They tax you on citizenship. If you renounce your citizenship for tax purposes, then the taxing authority, the Internal Revenue Service, will extend your citizenship for a further ten years, even if you moved to Gaza and took up a senior position with the Palestine Liberation Organization (PLO) or the Islamic Resistance Movement (Hamas) fighting the invasion of Palestine. Harry Truman said, "The buck stops here." The Internal Revenue Service says, "Most bucks stop here."

But, you can't even die to get away from the tax guys. There was a situation in Canada where a fellow left the country and established himself in the Bahamas, but he had not bothered to pay all of his departure tax.* He died and left some of his money to his relatives in Canada, and although his will was probated in the Bahamas, Canada Revenue Agency managed to step in and take back taxes from the heirs. Well, you may ask, didn't the heirs defend their position in the courts? Of course they did, but who pays the judges?

---

* When a person departs Canada, he is deemed to have disposed of all his assets and if there is any capital gains attributable to those he must pay capital gains tax.

It was all so depressing. Because of the government's financial situation, there would be unpleasant changes in my financial way of life, and I could not foresee what they would be and hence how to protect myself from them. All I knew for sure was that I would in some way be impoverished. What was really troublesome was that I had concluded, after listening to our resident economist, that the Canada Pension Plan was "toast" as was the money that was due to me from social security in the U.S. where I had worked for a time. All the plans, theirs and mine, were going broke. My old age would arrive and I would have given my nest egg to the tax man.

Angelo's solution of taking what was left and getting the hell out wouldn't work for me. I had a teenage daughter, a son, and a wife starting a new career. I was bound to be in the trenches for another ten years and to come up empty handed for my efforts.

I looked around me. My partners and colleagues were well into the debate. It was snowing outside and I had a long drive to Oakville. Some of the guys would get rooms in the Royal York Hotel and change into their spare suits at work rather than risk a drunken trip home on snow-covered roads. It was all so depressing, and if I didn't hurry, I'd be late for dinner to boot.

"Good night, guys. See you at eight, tomorrow."

CHAPTER 2

Buddy, Can You SPARE A PROZAC?

I took the elevator down to the parking garage and as I walked over to my pig iron I realized that it was on its last wheels and would have to be replaced next year. I would buy the same make and model, but now in an effort to keep prices down, the manufacturer was no longer putting on front disc brakes and some of the other features that I liked.

You can imagine how depressed I was. Old taxes, old car, and ageing me. I certainly wasn't going to continue reading *Tackling the Taxman* tonight. That tome outlined all of the illegal doings of the Canada Revenue Agency and how the *Income Tax Act* was used to benefit the friends and members of government and punish the ruling party's enemies.

Martha was preparing to serve dinner as I arrived, so at least that worked out. Duncan, our son, was lost in the Internet and his sister, Katherine, was continuing to attempt to grow a phone in her ear. Life was normal on the home front.

At dinner, I repeated some of the after-work conversation — the statistics on the high growth rate in the welfare industry and the debt problem. Katherine and Duncan immediately became quite interested in the dinner conversation, which was unusual.

Duncan said, "I hear the government wants to raise college and university fees because your generation has blown the budget. It's just going to make it that much tougher to go to university."

Katherine wasn't about to be left out. "I tried to price a ski trip for the school's ski club to Banff and do you know what the airport tax per person is? I thought that we paid for the airports through our taxes. Why do we have to pay a fee to use them?"

"Look," I said, "I don't want to hear any more about this. I had a great day at work until I listened to my partners tell me that your mother and I were going to spend our retirement in poverty because we had been taxed to death."

"I don't think it is at all fair that we should have to pay for your debts," complained Duncan.

"Our generation didn't just lavish ourselves. You and your sister did quite well out of the expenditures of the government. How many people your sister's age can afford to plan a ski trip half way across the country for the school ski club, part of which is subsidized by taxpayers?"

"Duncan's right. We didn't ask for any of this and now we are going to have to pay for it."

Just great. The government was not only going to start a racial schism in the country, it was also causing intergenerational strife. "Your generation's problems are simple compared to those of people like your mother and me. We have to worry about our old age. Who's going to pay for our pensions and our deteriorating health?"

"You should have been saving for your old age," said Duncan.

"How in the hell do you expect me to save for my old age when every marginal dollar I earn is taxed at 48 percent and every after-tax dollar I spend is taxed at 15 percent sales tax when I spend it? The government, on instituting the GST, promised us that there would be a break on income taxes to adjust for the sales tax, which I have yet to see, and a previous prime minister lied to us when he said he would abolish the sales tax. To make matters worse, if I do put some money into investments for old age, half of the investment earnings are taxed away."

"Well, if you're naïve enough to believe a politician's promise, then you certainly shouldn't be handling your own money," quipped Duncan.

"Dad, you can always put it into a Registered Retirement Savings Plan," Katherine suggested.

"Read the papers, Katy. Even those amounts are being restricted."

"I still think it is inappropriate for the sins of the father to be passed on," said Duncan.

"As for health," Katherine interjected, "perhaps there would be more money for knee replacements and heart operations if they stopped doing sex change operations at $25,000 a pop."

"I can't change any of those things. That's the government's responsibility," I said.

"People get the government that they deserve," Duncan retorted.

"I didn't vote for them."

"Well somebody did."

"It's worse than that, Stew, the government pensions are tapped out. It looks like we aren't even going to get the pension we paid for," my wife said.

"It can't be that bad," I said. "Let's talk about it later."

After we had done the dishes and the kids were in their rooms I asked Martha what she meant with her comment about the government pensions.

"I have been doing some research, Stew, and the numbers don't look good."

Martha had been a journalist before Duncan was born and she still knew how to get the information that counted. She had spent the day on the computer to come up with some sobering facts.

"It seems that our family of four is $128,000 in debt. That is in just straight-funded debt. In other words, this debt is the amount of money owed by the Government of Canada for which it has issued bonds, or, in other words, I.O.U.'s. Those I.O.U.'s are issued to people around the world. If the government wanted to pay off that debt, it could only do so by going to all of the inhabitants of the country and asking them for the funds to pay off the debtors. It is similar to credit cards, which can only be paid off by the cardholder (either by earning, stealing, or borrowing the money). In the end, the government's debts are the responsibility of its taxpayers. The government has no source of income other than taxes. This $128,000 figure is based on our total debt, our $700 billion federal and $260 billion provincial debt, divided by 30 mil-

lion people is $32,000 per person. However, if you con-
sider that only 20 million people are in the work force or
practising a profession and hence paying taxes, it comes to
about $48,000 per head or $192,000 for our family of four.
I then read from the Fraser Institute's reports that if you
include all the off-balance sheet financing of Canada Pension
Plan obligations, debts guaranteed, and obligations under
programs such as Medicare, it comes to about $100,000 per
head or $400,000 for our family."

"I've been hearing a lot of grumbling about the Canada
Pension Plan but I can't make any sense out of it. Some
people say it is funded and others tell me it's unfunded.
What is the truth?" I asked.

"Well, it's sort of funded. You see, Stew, what happens
with the contributions is that they are given to a group of
fund managers and they invest it in the Canadian
economy. The facts of life are that the best performing
market in the world over the past 100 years has been the
U.S. stock market and it returned in real terms, after inflation an average of 6 percent. If the funds coming into the
Canada Pension Plan had been invested in that economy
rather than super low interest government bonds there
would be a more fully funded pension scheme in place for
Canadians. As it stands the money managers have to make
up for the past under performance while investing in an
economy, the U.S., with a diminishing currency. What
they make on the portfolio they lose to the currency. If
they invest in the Canadian market to protect them from
the vagaries of the currency shifts, they'll find themselves
with a growth of closer to 4 percent, real. The last figures I
saw were for 2003 and they showed that the fund had $54
billion — enough for 2.5 years of payments. The slack is

being taken up by a 9.9 percent income tax.

"We will have some return from the plan as long as we keep both parents in a family working and we can bring in some skilled immigrants. The problem with immigrants is that they are economically driven. They aren't going to go to a place where they can't get richer. So the ones you end up with are the ones who can't make it somewhere else. They come for the benefits not for the liabilities. Net result is don't add your Canada Pension Plan benefits into your net wealth."

"Martha, you must be wrong. I remember hearing on the news that Canadians were the richest people in the world with something like $255,000 per person in assets according to the United Nations."

"That figure includes credits for clean air, sparkling water, and serenity, none of which will buy you a loaf of bread. According to Statistics Canada, each Canadian is really worth a total of $70,000. That figure was derived by taking the market value of all the assets in Canada, such as buildings, roads, and factories, including the harvestable trees and fish and anything else of monetary value, and then deducting the outstanding liabilities."

"So, you are telling me that after 18 years of marriage the total value of our home, assets, and pension is a lousy $140,000? The cottage we are selling is worth $100,000 alone and it's paid for. What about our $200,000 in mutual funds?"

"Stew, you are talking about an individual basis and you are not factoring in our share of the country's debts. But, things will look better when your uncle Harry in Ireland dies. He said you will get a quarter of what's left in his estate."

"That'll help," I said "but the tax boys will get their hands on any benefits we may derive from that as well."

"Not necessarily," she said. "When we received that letter from your uncle's solicitors in England, they asked how we wanted our portion of the inheritance structured. That got me thinking and I called Linda, Paul's wife, and she said that he knew of ways we could keep the inheritance offshore and have it grow tax free. I told her you would call Paul tonight."

Paul was a tax lawyer who lived down the street. He tackled tax law like a Jesuit confronting the devil. He once told me that he felt that any dime that was paid in taxes just contributed to greater rot of the country's moral fabric.

I called him and asked if there was anything that could be done about Uncle Harry's legacy. He asked if Harry was a Canadian resident to which I replied that he lived in Ireland. Paul said we should speak. I asked him if he wanted to play a game of squash on Saturday afternoon at the Toronto Racquet Club in downtown Toronto. He agreed.

I chose the Toronto Racquet Club because it is downtown and, therefore, central and also because it is small. It is limited to 200 members and as such I know everybody. There was no chance that I would be overheard by somebody I didn't know. When it came to personal taxation, I was paranoid.

On Saturday, we played three games of soft-ball, of which I lost two, and therefore ended up paying for the shandies (a mixture of ginger beer and lager). We went up to the lounge and started sipping our thirst-quenching drinks.

"Tell me about Uncle Harry," Paul said.

"Uncle Harry was a vulture. He would look for companies in the U.S. that were failing and buy a stake in their shares at a very depressed price. He would then interest a venture fund or merchant bank into taking control of the company. If the new managers were able to turn the operation around, he would make a very substantial amount of money. If the company failed, the new owners would often use the remnant corporate shell for some other undertaking and Harry would do okay. Somehow he set up his operation so that he didn't pay any taxes. As a result, he became quite wealthy. In his later years, he gave up business and dedicated himself to pleasure. He was often seen in the more pleasant places of the world with very pleasant companions. On his 65th birthday, he started preparing for his eventual demise and his will. About a month ago, I got a letter from a firm of solicitors in England asking me how I wanted to structure my portion of Harry's legacy. What did they mean by that?"

"Either Harry or his solicitor is very tax-astute. You told me that Harry didn't pay any taxes. I suspect that is why he moved to Ireland. He structured his residency and his business operations in such a way that he was not liable for Irish income tax. He probably had no income in Ireland but substantial earnings offshore. Having made the effort to earn his money tax free, it sounds like he wants to provide his inheritors with the same benefits. His lawyers realize that you can receive your inheritance in any number of ways, some of which are more tax benign than others. For example, you could take your inheritance in a trust or some sort of offshore vehicle that could reduce or eliminate the taxes that would be earned by the inherited money. Let me give you an example.

"If your inheritance were given to you as the beneficiary of a trust set up by your uncle at his death and the trustees were in the Bahamas or Bermuda and the trust established there, then the earnings of the trust would be tax free when you took them into your hands."

I felt myself salivating. It wasn't just the inheritance but the whole idea of using trusts to shield my investment income until needed that was exciting. I could move the $200,000 savings Martha and I had in mutual funds into a trust and the government couldn't touch it or its earnings. I said as much to Paul and asked when we could get going on it.

"It's not that easy," he said. "Your uncle Harry falls under a special circumstance. Let me explain the position of trusts in the Canadian and American tax scene. First you have to know the jargon.

"The person who puts assets in the trust is the settlor or in U.S. parlance, the grantor. The person who administers those assets is the trustee. The recipient of the benefits of the trust is the beneficiary. Occasionally, the term 'protector' is used. This is a person who oversees the trustees to make sure the beneficiary's interests are being pursued."

"That seems redundant," I said. "Ostensibly, the trustees are looking after the assets for the best interests of the beneficiaries. Why would you need a protector as well?"

"Think about commercial law, Stew. The function of a judgement in commercial courts against the defendant is to cause him to undertake something he is unwilling to do. In the case where the grantor or settlor of a trust has the ability to influence the trustees, a court could provide a decision forcing the settlor to direct the trustees in a manner he did not condone. In that case, the protector would see the court ruling as harmful to the trust and remove the trustees and take whatever action necessary to protect the trust's assets."

"How could I be forced to do something detrimental to my own trust?" I asked.

"Supposing you were kidnapped and the terms of your release required that the trust pay over its assets to a kidnapper. The protector would not allow the trustees to take such action even if you directed them to do so while under duress."

"Paul, we are looking at a trust to avoid taxes so your example is unrealistic. The tax department isn't going to kidnap me."

"Really, Stew? What if the tax department got a court order for you to direct the trustees to pay all of the trust assets to them? If you disobeyed the court order, you would be in contempt of court and taken to jail and held there until the appropriate amount was deposited with the court. Is that not kidnapping?

"Now let's suppose you are in jail and you obey the court order and send a letter to the trustees to pay out the assets of the trust to the court. The protector, upon viewing that letter, would not allow the trustees to hand over the assets to the court.

"Therefore, you have obeyed the court's direction and must be freed. The kidnappers have held you and then released you because they can't get what they want. In Bermuda, the protector is used to stop the trust from acting under duress. In the Bahamas, the trust laws have a ruling that prohibits the trustees from acting under any instruction that seems to be from duress."

"That all seems so intellectually elegant," I said. "Who thought out this system?"

"It evolved. You see, trusts got their real development during the Crusades. The nobleman heading off to free

Palestine from the infidels had to worry about the care and management of his estate while he was gone and the possibility that he might not return. Therefore, he would put the care of his assets in the hands of someone he could trust — the trustee. The duress wrinkle was added after the creation of the transit tax. The crusaders had to pass through central Europe on their way to the holy lands and the owners of those lands found a new source of income. They would demand payment for such things as the use of the Danube River. If you didn't pay your transit tax, you were provided with room and board in their dungeon. The duress wrinkle was added to trusts to end the practice of kidnapping under any guise. So trusts and taxes have had an association since their beginnings.

"Now let's look at the structure of income tax. A Canadian or U.S. taxpayer is responsible for all his worldwide income regardless of the source. Therefore, if you own offshore assets and these generate earnings, then the income from the assets is taxable in your hands. Most tax avoidance structures are based on removing the stigma of asset ownership from the individual and placing that onerous obligation in the hands of an entity that will pay no tax. At the same time, the individual maintains control over the assets while having given up title.

"When taxes start to rise in any country, taxpayers will begin to look for a haven for their capital and earnings. When you see taxes rising on income, you can rest assured that a levy on assets is not far behind. This gave rise to the popularity of the 'Bahamian and Bermudian Trusts.' Rich Canadians or Americans would settle their assets in trusts administered by trustees in the islands with the settlors or their dependents as the long term beneficiaries. So, let's say that a million dollars is put in the trust as capital. In the first year, it earns $100,000. If none of the money is paid out, the trust will have $1,100,000 in capital the following year. Earnings of a trust that are not paid out become capital. When the time comes for the trust to pay out, the funds that are received by the beneficiaries would be almost completely capital and therefore tax free."

"Why is that, Paul?"

"Because very few countries tax the movement of capital. They only tax earnings. Therefore, if the trust is all capital, there is no income tax to be paid on the capital transfer from the trust to the beneficiary."

"Why didn't the government tax the earnings of the trust in the first place?"

"The trustees and the trust were domiciled in the Bahamas or in Bermuda, which under normal trust law means that the trust is Bahamian or Bermudian and only taxable by those governments, which have no income tax on trusts. Therefore, the U.S. or Canadian governments couldn't tax what was not residing in their countries."

"That's what I want, Paul, a Bermudian Trust."

"Sorry, Stewart, those days are gone. You see, the governments of Canada and the U.S. saw all that potential money for pork barrelling being shielded and decided to pursue it. They made up rules to thwart the use of trusts. In the case of a U.S. resident, the trust's income is considered to be the grantor's and hence any earnings would be taxable in the U.S. In Canada, if the settlor of a trust is a resident of Canada, then the trust is resident in Canada and hence taxable in Canada."

"What do the governments do? Look at every trust to see if its grantor or settlor is North American?"

"One of the great advantages of trusts, Stew, is that they are not registered or listed anywhere, and neither the taxers nor the beneficiaries know that they exist until there is a distribution."

"How do the Americans get around this problem of the grantor having to accept the tax liability?" I asked.

"The trust companies have devised structures such that the grantor's trust does not receive the income from the assets until instructed. In that way, the grantor can determine when and where he wants to receive the income. If the trust receives the assets at the time of the death of the grantor then there is no one to tax."

"Tell me, Paul, haven't these changes to the tax laws regarding trusts ruined your legal business?"

"No. Think about what the rules say, 'If the settlor is a Canadian resident, then the trust is taxable in Canada.' Take your uncle Harry. If he leaves your portion of the inheritance in a trust, then because he, the settlor, is not a Canadian resident, the trust would not be deemed resident in Canada because the trustees and the location of the trust are all foreign. You would only pay tax on the earnings of the trust if you were to take them into your hands. However, if you were clever, you would never take out the current year's earnings but rather the past year's, which are considered untaxed capital.

"Also, consider people immigrating to Canada. At the time that they settle a trust, they are not residents of Canada. Therefore, you have a grey area. There is also a provision in the immigration rules that allows immigrants to shield their assets from tax by putting them in trusts for five years from the day of landing. To take it a step further, what if you sold all your assets to a foreign corporation that you did not control, and that corporation then settled a trust on you and your descendants. As you can see, Stewart, there are all sorts of trust vehicles that can be set up with any number of wrinkles. However, the thing to remember is the rule about the settlor not being a Canadian resident and that none of the assets in a trust was owned by a resident of Canada."

"Why don't you hear more about trusts?" I asked.

"You will in the future. The tax department has singled out trusts as the barn door they want to close now that the billion-dollar horses have fled. Under the existing laws, you could follow in the footsteps of the Bronfman family.

"You could exchange your assets that had appreciated greatly in price for shares of a private company issued to you by a trust. Because it was a share swap, no capital gains tax would be generated. The trust could then move to the U.S. and there would still be no tax triggered because the value of its assets was basically unchanged from the date of acquisition. Tax would only be incurred in Canada if the trust sold the assets before ten years. However, if the trust sold the assets after ten years, the beneficiaries would only be liable for U.S. tax at a very benign rate, and if they were no longer residents in Canada or the U.S., tax might be avoided completely.

"This type of activity and the growing use of trusts has led to legislation being proposed that would require Canadians to report on their income tax form if they are beneficiaries of a trust, if they have received loans from a trust, or if they have put assets into a trust. As it stands now, the taxers want to classify a beneficiary as someone who has received a payout from a trust. There are rumours that the reporting may be extended to beneficiaries who have not yet received income. That, of course, smacks of terminal stupidity because there is no way that anyone can be sure that he is not a beneficiary. Under this scenario, every Canadian would have to answer 'possibly' to avoid filing a false income tax return. The other question that hasn't been answered is whether or not the tax department has the right to ask you questions about anything except your income. As things stand now, the answer is no.

"Also, there are many trusts that originate from desires other than tax avoidance. Let's say you are an Ontario doctor. You've just been told that the Ontario Health Insurance Program is no longer going to subsidize doctors' malpractice insurance. The next day you read in the paper that because the provincial legal-aid program has been providing legal services for indigent drunk drivers and impoverished squabbling couples the program is broke."

"Hold it just a minute," I said. "Are you telling me that people who have enough money to buy cars and booze are claiming that they are too poor to defend themselves against a drunk driving charge?"

"It seems so, Stew. Apparently, it is the right of all Canadians to own a car, to get drunk, and to go out on the road to kill someone. It is felt to be elitist to reserve that right for only the self-sufficient or rich. Therefore, the lawyers who have been living off the legal-aid program by defending these party animals are going to have to fend for themselves now. The easiest way to encourage this new self-sufficiency is to allow these lawyers to take cases on a contingency fee basis. This means that lawyers are going to have to generate their own clientele. The era of fast-track ambulance chasing has arrived. We will now see a new era in which doctors will be paying tremendous insurance premiums to protect their assets, and at the same time, a cadre of lawyers will be chasing aggrieved patients with promises of instant riches as potential clients. It is a formula for economic disaster for the doctor.

"The doctors do have a possible defence. I have been setting up 'Asset Protection Trusts' for them. The doctors place the ownership of their assets in the trust, thus leaving themselves with no assets in their name should they be sued and lose. Doctors could then arrange for lower coverage on their malpractice insurance because they have less to protect. If they get sued and lose, the malpractice insurance will cover the legal costs but their assets are in a trust for their spouses and children. The plaintiff in the case has won a pyrrhic victory in that he has a judgement in his favour but no financial gain from the exercise. In fact, in areas of the U.S. where doctors have taken to the use of asset protection trusts, the number of malpractice suits has fallen."

"Why is that, Paul?"

"If one of my partners in the malpractice specialty is visited by a potential client asking him to take on a contingency fee based malpractice case, the first thing my partner will do is a credit check and balance-sheet assessment of the doctor. If the doctor has only a few assets and little in the way of malpractice insurance because of an asset protection trust, then my partner will ask for a retainer before taking the case. When the client asks why the retainer is necessary, seeing as his case is ironclad and the doctor indefensible, my partner will explain that the case will definitely be decided for the plaintiff and with a very large settlement; however, the problem will be in the collecting of that judgement because the doctor has no attachable assets, as they have been placed beyond the court's reach in a trust.

"Therefore, the enquiries about trusts could swamp the tax sleuths with more information than they can handle as people report all sorts of trusts as well as tax-avoidance vehicles."

"Are you saying that trusts as a tax-avoidance device are finished?"

"No, Stewart. The structures will change and become more complicated to accommodate any new tax rulings. Without seeming to feather my own nest, I would recommend that you get the advice of a Canadian, and I stress Canadian, tax lawyer to help you with your uncle's inheritance. You don't want a trust set up by some foreign lawyer who is only moderately up to date on Canadian tax law. Remember that a lawyer in the Bahamas has no licence to lose in Canada if he should provide you with bad advice. As well, who is going to go to bat for you if Canada Revenue Agency comes calling?"

"Wait a minute Paul. What's this about new tax rulings?"

"In the late 1990s the Government became paranoid about Canadians' potential to protect themselves from high and rising taxes by use of the offshore. So they enunciated a suite of new rules and laws to be included in the *Income Tax Act*. That was the year 2000. It was soon discovered that many of the government's friends and party contributors would be caught by the changes. The Bronfman Trust to move their assets out of the country tax free and Paul Martin's offshore shipping empire would all be paying huge amounts of tax. The ability of those friends to be able to contribute to the Liberal party's coffers would have been severely handicapped. Changing the Tax Act at that time was considered a sacrifice too great for the Liberal Party of Canada to make for the coffers of government. Also some of the ideas in the legislation were plain goofy. The drafters of the new legislation had given the Canadian government the power to tax foreign trusts wherever they might reside. I wonder how they expected to collect. The new rules were never enacted but remain pending. It is doubtful any government would be willing to promulgate them now.

"A lot of people looked at the legislation and its silliness and concluded that the real object of the proposals was not to implement them but to scare Canadians away from the offshore. To some extent that effect has worked.

"So, Paul, you're saying I should establish a Canadian trust."

"Not so. If I, a Canadian lawyer, were setting up your trust I would probably do it in the Turks and Caicos Islands. The reason being that many countries like Canada have a rule against the perpetuity of trust. This means that after a certain period the trust has to be wound down. In Canada, after 18 years you have to dissolve the trust so that the tax boys can take a run at it. The Turks and Caicos not only allow perpetual trusts but they have taken the best aspects of the Bahamian and Bermudian trust structures as well.

"But before you do decide to do something, you should determine what you want and try to keep it simple because trusts are not cheap to set up. Be prepared to pay between $6,000 and $10,000 to set one up. In the U.S., it can be even more expensive because of the intricacies and the fact that assets have to be managed outside of the grantor's trust. If you can save big tax dollars or protect a lot of assets, it is worthwhile."

There were certain things that bothered me about the trust concept. The most important was that someone else would be administering the assets, although I could probably provide some direction to the trustees as to how the funds should be invested. But then, as I understood Paul, the closer I got to managing the assets the more I looked like one of the trustees, and the harder it would be for me to justify the arrangement to Canada Revenue Agency. The other problem was CRA's recent interest in the subject. How far could they go in their probing? But then, this whole idea of tax avoidance struck me as something in which I should get more involved. It looked like it could be the growth industry of the next decade. I may be on to the next great wave — this generation's Hula Hoop. I still had concerns about the legality of all this and with a lawyer at my table, what better time to ask.

"Paul, isn't some of this stuff illegal?"

"No. You have to distinguish between tax avoidance and tax evasion. It is the evasion that is illegal. But then, speaking of legalities, you should be aware that the greatest use of illegal methods is by the tax department itself."

"I can't believe that. Are you telling me that our government would do something illegal?"

"Exactly. Last month, I had a case dissolve that looked like a sure thing. A doctor had called me with the usual tale of woe. It seems that some four years ago his accountant had screwed up and it was discovered last year. He paid the reassessment, back taxes, and interest and he thought that the case was closed. Not so. The guy is a naturopath and charges for his services. As well, he is a member of the Church of Scientology, which might have led to his being singled out for harassment. Two months ago, out of the blue, the tax cowboys sent letters to all the stockbrokers in Toronto asking if he had an account and they put injunctions on his bank accounts, liens against his property, and a lien against the receipts of the charge-card payments from his patients.

"My thoughts immediately turned to former prime minister Brian Mulroney who, when the Royal Canadian Mounted Police sent letters to Swiss banks asking if he had an account, sued the government for $50 million for defamation. I thought to heck with the tax case. I could make the guy rich on the basis of Mulroney's suit. If Brian won, then we would win. I brought it up at a partners' meeting and everybody agreed it was a sure thing and that the defamation guys should start to work on it."

"What happened? How did you lose the client?"

"Well, the doctor had a well-known investigative journalist as a patient. When she heard about the case, she asked if the doctor would mind if she wrote it up as an article. The doctor is as transparent as a window and right up front. 'Sure. That would be nice,' says he. The journalist called the doctor's wife, who did all his bookkeeping, and asked whom they were dealing with at CRA. When the wife told her, the journalist had a release drawn up allowing her to inquire into the tax affairs of the doctor. It was addressed to the case worker and signed by the doctor and his wife. When the journalist went down to the tax office with her release in hand, there was a near panic. They told her to come back tomorrow. That night she got a call from the doctor's wife-bookkeeper, asking her to drop the article because the tax department had done a recent assessment and found that everything was in order and that all the injunctions would be lifted."

"I didn't think they could work that fast," I said.

"I know what happened. The local office administrator

could see a dog's breakfast developing right before his eyes with the attendant magazine articles and he decided to run rather than fight."

"Why would he do that?"

"Think about it, Stew. When have you ever seen a news report in the papers about the tax office screwing up and having to pay court costs et cetera? Never,* although I know it does happen. The only thing you see in the news is that doctor so and so was found to have evaded some amount of tax, has been prosecuted by the tax department, and a pound of his flesh has been extracted. Those news items are released to the papers in March, at tax time, with lots of local colour to scare the living Jesus out of anybody thinking of non-compliance. Can you imagine what a story about the incompetence or impotence of the tax department would do to collections? It would be similar to the collection plate at a Baptist meeting after the minister revealed that the devil died yesterday in a plane crash."

"How did you lose the client?"

"I talked to the doctor the next day and said that we would be filing papers for suit similar to Brian Mulroney's. He asked me to wait before doing so and then called me back the next day to say that he would prefer that I not proceed. When I asked why, he said that the tax department was considering an audit and it might occur if we, as a legal firm, were pursuing a case against them."

"That seems odd," I said.

"Not really. You see many people when filling out their

---

* This is no longer the case as I have recently published a book detailing the illegal activities and failures of CRA. It is *Tackling the Taxman* available at your local bookstore or from www.Alexdoulis.com.

tax form consciously or subconsciously expand their costs and shrink their income so as to report the lowest taxable income. Was the amount of business automobile mileage correct or did it include some personal miles? What about that convention in Paradise? Would it be considered real or would there be the devil to pay? So, everyone wants to forego any scrutiny of their tax form. The word 'audit' strikes terror in the hearts of the taxpayer and many stories are planted in the press to maintain that image."

"That's hardly illegal," I said.

"It is a crime to threaten people to extract money.* The use of threats and the wholesale imposition of injunctions, which are costly to remove, constitute a near if not certain criminal activity. Think about it. If I went to you and said that unless you gave me money I would stop your access to your bank account, you would call the police."

"But those actions are taken as a result of a debt," I said.

"Wrong on two counts, Stew. If the tax cowboys figure you may owe them money, then they'll strike first and settle later. It's easier that way for them. Also, it is not a debt. A debt is an amount of money owing as a result of the receipt of goods or services."

This was getting scary. I was listening to a tax lawyer telling me that the taxing authorities would violate the country's laws. "No," I said, "they must be just enforcing the laws that are passed by Parliament and subject to the rule of law."

"Stew, you still don't understand. The *Income Tax Act* in Canada and the 16th amendment to the U.S. Constitution allowing the taxation of incomes are probably illegal. They

* See previous footnote.

both appear to violate the rights guaranteed under the founding documents of the two countries.

"In both countries, tax authorities can act preemptively if they can make the case that taxpayers may abscond with their assets before the tax authorities can get their hands on them. This tying up of assets is used by the tax department to enforce collection. 'Pay us or you'll never see your bank account again.' Do you consider that just? What if I re-phrase it — 'You giva me your money or you no see your son Giuseppe ever again.' It is pure and simple extortion.

"Also, both countries have different rates of taxation for different groups of people. Let's suppose that the govern-ment passed a law taxing all left-handed people at a higher rate than right-handed people. There would be a great public outcry. However, it is considered quite acceptable to have different rates of taxation for different earnings groups."

"How can they get away with that sort of thing?"

"Stewart, they are collecting the funds necessary to keep the politicians in their jobs. Do you expect a politician to uphold your rights when by doing so he might cut into the amount of money he has to distribute? No consideration of natural justice is allowed to interfere with that process. Remember that three billion dollars of political patronage has to be paid for."

"But, even that must come to an end sometime," I said.

"Stew, it did end in Italy — they ran out of patronage positions. So, the politicians had to find a new way to buy votes. They did it with phony state benefits. A random check in Palermo, Sicily, turned up the fact that 42 people being paid disability pensions for total blindness had driver's licences and one was a licensed television cameraman for the state-owned television station. It was determined that after running out of patronage positions a new form of quid pro quo had to be found for the political fixers. Voilà! State pension money.

"You need hard cash to pay for an elected position in most countries. It comes out of our pockets and any abuse of our laws is justifiable to collect the most money possible. Take the social insurance number for example. Every Canadian must have one. When the act establishing the social insurance number was debated in Parliament, the opposition fought it on the basis that it would be used to form a big-brother type state where all the citizens could be traced by their number. The ruling party of the time insisted that the number was only to keep accounts for the payment of social benefit entitlements, such as pensions. They, therefore, included in the law a fine of $5,000 for the use of the number for anything but an account number for benefits. You couldn't even ask for someone's social insurance number. But now, when you open a bank account, make a credit card application, or open a stock account, you are asked for your social insurance number, illegally. Why? Because the very thing that the opposition parties feared decades ago has come to pass. Canada Revenue Agency is using your social insurance number as your tax account number and cross-correlating all your financial activities through your social insurance number."

"That sounds sort of sinister."

"It gets worse. Have you ever heard of the ACSES files?"*

* I obtained, through the access to information rules my own ACSES file for the 11 years 1990–2001 during which I was non-resident and hence not subject to tax in Canada. It was thicker than the Toronto phone book and contained amongst other trivia poorly executed reviews of my books.

"No. What the hell is that?"

"It's where the Feds keep all the information on us, especially financial. With your social insurance number, the tax department can trace every financial movement you've ever made. Now remember, according to the *Income Tax Act*, you are only required to report your income. In your ACSES file, they keep track of your other financial activities."

"That's sleazy," I said.

"No, it gets worse. The tax department manipulates the rules. They have a rule that says if you play to win the tax game, then automatically you lose. You are not allowed to win. This comes about from section 245 of the *Income Tax Act* also known as GAAR, the General Anti-Avoidance Rule. This says that if you undertake a commercial activity whose only result is to decrease your tax burden, then the tax department has the right to annul the transaction."

"Paul, you are really confusing me. All along you have been telling me that tax avoidance is legal, and now you are trying to tell me that the tax department has a rule that stops you from avoiding tax. That rule gets violated every year by most Canadian investors who sell shares at a loss to offset their gains. How do they get away with it?"

"The reason that the investing public can violate the rule is that section 245 is probably illegal because tax avoidance is not unlawful. You see, the tax gunslingers threaten taxpayers with GAAR and they usually capitulate. However, those who have good tax lawyers or know the rules will say 'Go ahead, prosecute me under 245. Let's see what happens.' What happens is the gunslingers holster their guns and offer to make up and be friends. The reason being, Stew, is that back in 1936, the famous Westminster v. the

Inland Revenue case was tried in the highest court of the land in England, the House of Lords. Lord Tomlin ruled, 'a man had the right to arrange his financial matters in such a manner as to incur the minimum amount of tax.' That ruling was never overturned, and because Canada was subject to British law at that time, the rule applies in Canada also. Therefore, GAAR, which flies directly in the face of Westminster v. the Inland Revenue, would probably be thrown out if it ever reached the courts in Canada."*

"Well, why in the hell doesn't somebody do something about it?" I asked.

"You have to have someone willing and able to go to court as a plaintiff before the case can be heard. If there is one aspect of GAAR that Canada Revenue Agency wants to avoid, it is scrutiny by the courts in light of the British precedent. Therefore, as I said, if you confront Canada Revenue Agency on GAAR with regard to income tax, they will offer to give up their old gunslinging ways and become law-abiding citizens. They don't want a shootout at the 'Last Dollar' saloon. But once your back is turned, they will continue to threaten other people with what they know is probably illegal. If they go to court and lose, then the ability to threaten is gone. As long as no one challenges them, the fact that they are using a rubber gun as a weapon will never be known.

"So, who is going to be the white hat-wearing sheriff to take on the bandits? If you think about it, you'll note that

---

* The recent Singleton and Bouelle cases showed that GAAR was inapplicable. Singleton was heard in the Supreme Court of Canada and Bouelle in the Federal Tax Court. After the SCC ruling on Singleton, the Tax Court had difficulty in ruling for CRA in tax avoidance.

there is no unified body to fight tax abuses. The Legal-Aid Plan is there to protect people from unpalatable marriages but does not come to the assistance of abused taxpayers. The Canadian Civil Liberties Union will fight to the death for you to jeopardize your physical safety in any manner you feel ethnically justifiable, such as wearing a turban rather than a hard hat on the job, but ignores the fact that real liberty also includes the right to enjoy the fruits of your labour and the guarantee of your right to property."

"Okay, so the General Anti-Avoidance Rule is kind of questionable but I doubt that there are other unreasonable laws in the hands of Canada Revenue Agency," I said.

"Consider this. If you were to beat me to death with that squash racquet because of your anger over the wonderful game I just played and then run home, the police would have to convince a judge to issue a search warrant that is only good in daylight hours in order to enter your house to look for the weapon of my demise. However, if the tax cowboys think that you may not have reported all your income, they won't get a search warrant, they'll use an off-the-shelf 'writ of assistance,' which allows them to break into your home at any time of the day or night to look for tax material. So, in the eyes of the government, tax evasion is a more heinous crime than murder."

"That appears to me to be totally unjust," I replied. "I believe that our courts would never allow that sort of thing."

"Really, Stew? What about the Del Zotto case.* The Supreme Court of Canada ruled that it was acceptable to

* See the *Globe and Mail,* January 22, 1999.

violate Mr. Del Zotto's constitutional rights based on the argument that the government of Canada was highly dependant on taxation.

"No, it's not unjust. It's criminal.* But our country was founded on the concept of criminal activity being a cornerstone. Remember our first prime minister's request to the railway tycoons, 'Send me another 10,000,' and when they did he gave them the best lands and a major portion of the mineral rights of this country. Nothing's changed."

"That sort of thing could never happen today."

"Really? Brian Mulroney was given the senior job at the Iron Ore Company of Canada while he was waiting to get into politics. What does a lawyer know about running an iron ore company? Or how about his successor Jean Chrétien, a Quebec politician. While out of office, he was paid $50,000 per year by Gordon Capital as a consultant. Gordon Capital had no offices in Quebec and only dealt with a dozen or so Quebec institutional clients through its Toronto office. What consulting services could a man whose only capabilities were in Quebec politics provide to a Toronto-based institutional brokerage firm?

"In the end, it may not have been in vain that Gordon Capital and Mr. Chrétien enjoyed each other's company because as you know when it came time to privatize Petro-Canada, the job was given to Gordon Capital."

"That's not so odd," I said. "During the rounds of privatizations, lots of brokerage companies got the business."

---

* The CRA so abused the rights of a Mr. Cowell that Judge Lenz had to throw out a charge of hiding $300,000 of income because of the illegal actions of CRA. See Brantford, Ontario Court file 95-3100 or *Globe and Mail* January 2001 edition.

"Sure they did. But how much of that business was dispensed on an auction basis? The legitimate way that privatizations should be done is through auctions. The government should offer its share holdings to the highest bidder and the underwriter who buys the shares would then perform the chore for which his organization originated and that is to distribute stock to the public. Also, when viewing privatizations, remember that one of the objectives is to distribute the stock as broadly as possible so that the greatest number of citizens end up with shares. Gordon Capital had no retail clients. It only dealt with large institutional investors, such as pension and mutual funds. How many small investors would Gordon Capital be offering the shares to? None.

"Remember that every time the government gives something away to some privileged group, it will come out of your pocket. To get into your pocket, the government needs the tax system. To make it work requires the ruthlessness and contempt of the Gestapo."

"There must be a way out," I said. "I am sure other countries are not so draconian in their pursuit of tax revenue."

"I hope you are not thinking of our cousins to the south. The American tax authorities are as bad or worse. In the U.S., when they want to use the legal rubber hose on the reluctant taxpayer, they trot out the anti-racketeering RICO act. This was never meant for use in the tax field, but because it so successfully ties up the individual it is routinely used for the shakedown."

Maybe it was the dull dreariness of Toronto in January that was depressing me and all those around me. Perhaps a week in Florida might put all this in a better light. I really didn't want to hear anymore. It seemed that the tax system in Canada was set up in such a way that one's rights could be violated and natural justice ignored. The sense of despair was enough to send you on a Prozac bender. I was about to ask Paul if there was any way out of the tax gulag when a couple of guys came over and asked us if we wanted to play some doubles. I felt so angry and frustrated that the opportunity to abuse a squash ball seemed the most therapeutic exercise possible. We played and won.

CHAPTER 3

Of Trusts AND TRUSSES

When I got home from my squash game, I found that Martha was in a good mood. She was playing some old 1940s music and singing in the kitchen.

"Sweetheart," I said, "You've got the words wrong. The song goes:

'Just Molly and me,
And baby makes three,
We're happy in my blue heaven.'"

"No, Stewart, you've got the words wrong. They are:

'Just money and me,
And bonds makes three,
We're happy in my blue haven.'"

"That doesn't make any sense," I said.

"It would if you had spent the afternoon as I did, reading *Take Your Money and Run!* instead of belching and sweating in that bastion of male chauvinism."

"I've told you before that I'll put you up for membership at the Toronto Racquet Club when you get me into that hotbed of female chauvinism, The Verity Club."

This had always been a running joke of ours, as my wife, who was a humanist rather than a feminist, believed that all people should be treated equally and that women should, therefore, be admitted to my males-only squash club, while I insisted that I be allowed into her women-only social and athletic club. "In any case, Angelo's remedy to the Canadian taxation system was to give up his Canadian residency to become a resident in a country that had no tax on foreign-source income and then live off his bond interest, which came from outside of his country of residence. Are you prepared to move all of us to Ireland or Greece?"

"You obviously didn't read the part about tax havens," she replied.

"That's kind of complicated and requires a lot of money. Anyway, what were you doing reading that book again? Dreaming of escape?"

"No. Guess who's in town? Angelo. He has come to do some promotional lectures and for some surgery from his long-time practitioner."

"He can't get treated in Canada. He's not a resident, and anyway, if it's elective surgery he'll have to wait months."

"Wrong, Stew. It is elective surgery and he goes in for it next week. He's a cash-paying customer. Things move faster for them."

"It'll cost him a mint."

"Wrong again. Remember, he has private insurance for about $3,000 a year in premiums."

"How come you know so much?" I snorted, somewhat miffed.

"Research. I was talking to the ladies in the locker room and who should enter but Angelo's wife, Sarah. They're coming for dinner next week on Thursday and I decided to review Angelo's book to brush up on tax havens."

"That's not research; that is serendipity. Anyway, I'm going to look at the book and see if there is anything useful before we see Ang."

I found the old dog-eared book and went to the section on tax havens. There was much written between the lines that had not been expanded upon and unless you knew the tax system, it didn't make much sense. We still had an old phone number for Angelo in Toronto. On the off chance, I dialed. When the phone was answered, I thought I could smell the aroma of Monte Cristo cigars over the line. He was an inveterate cigar smoker. He had stopped smoking ten years ago as a result of his wife's concerns about his throat, but now that he was diagnosed as having colitis, an inflammation of the colon, he was smoking again. It seems that nicotine is a palliative for the affliction.

"Angelo?"

"Who did you expect?"

"Ang, it's Stewart. Martha saw Sarah at Verity and invited you for dinner on Thursday, but I've got some questions about taxes. Could you help me?"

"Stew, I'm always ready to help anybody escape from tyranny but you're too young to leave."

"I don't want to leave. Martha says I should brush up on tax havens."

"We can talk, but not over the phone. Someone is listening on this line."

"How do you know?" I asked.

"When you hang up it will take about six seconds for the connection to break. I figure that's the time it takes for the tape recorder on the line to shut down. I've complained and told the recorder that I'm not going to say anything incriminating on the line but they still haven't removed it. Anyway, what I talk about is purely legal but I figure they might use the phone information to harass people. So, let's get together tomorrow afternoon. Are you still a member at Toronto Racquet? If so, let's shoot some pool and chat."

"Good idea. How about 2:00 p.m.?"

"Done," he said.

At dinner that night, Martha asked me what I had learned from Paul.

"I found out about trusts," I said.

"Gee, Dad, I didn't know you had a hernia," quipped Duncan.

"Don't be smart or clean your ears. I said trusts not truss. If you know what's good for your financial future, you'd better brush up as well. Your great uncle Harry is about to croak in Ireland and he may leave this family some untaxed money. That, for your untutored mind, is about twice as much as taxed money. You may yet go to college without becoming a pauper in the process."

"But Daddy, everybody should pay taxes," said our daughter.

"Of course, dearest, but how much? Last year your mother and I paid over $80,000 in income taxes not to mention sales and property taxes for probably another $15,000. Could you be so kind as to tell me what we got for it?"

"You got health care," she said.

"Yeah, well that cost the government $2,500 per Canadian. That means that as a family we cost $10,000 to support for health care. Where did the other $85,000 go?"

"There's national defence you know," she retorted.

"Defence? From whom? The Mohawk Indians? Katherine, give it up. There is no way you're going to find that this family consumed even half the amount we paid in taxes."

"There is no way out so why are we even talking about this?" asked Duncan.

"Well, my boy, if you spent more time on the Internet looking for tax information rather than observing the fine points of female anatomy, you might learn about trusts and tax havens. For instance, trusts can be used to shield assets from seizure, or in special cases, to protect income from taxation. Also, Angelo tells me that corporate structures in tax havens have taken over where trusts left off. There is a whole universe of tax avoidance just waiting to unfold."

"Does that mean we are not going to have to pay any more taxes?" asked Katherine.

"No, Katy, but we will be able to pay our fair share and nothing more."

"What's our fair share? The minimum tax?"

"If it were my choice, we wouldn't have a minimum tax without a maximum. How many people consume $100,000 of government services? Yet there are many people paying those kinds of taxes. However, when you have a minimum and maximum tax, what you are really talking about is a flat tax. That of course is democratic. Everybody would pay the same percentage of their income to the government like they do in Hong Kong or Estonia. The whole idea of graduated tax is undemocratic. You can either say you are denying the poor the opportunity to support their country to the extent the rich are or you are penalizing the rich because they are more productive than the poor. In either case, someone is being discriminated against."

I could see Duncan was having revelations as he slurped his linguini with clam sauce. Katherine on the other hand was beginning to pout. She believed that the middle class was going to lift the poor out of poverty by their boot straps. However, I couldn't convince her that although the effort had been underway for three generations, there were people who were born into the dole and government housing, who would die on the dole and in government housing, following in the footsteps of their parents and grandparents, and there was nothing we could do to change that.

"Gee, that's discrimination," said Duncan. "The tax department is violating people's right to be treated equally. That's unfair. Go get 'em, Dad."

Well, at least I had one convert. I doubted Katherine would accept the thesis. She knew what she believed and refused to be confused by facts. She proved true to my analysis of her. "Daddy, if the rich don't pay lots of taxes, the poor will starve. There will be riots in the streets."

"Not really, sweetheart. Maybe their quantity or quality of life might diminish but then again maybe some of them might seek work, and Kim at our local convenience store would be able to find someone willing to work the night shift and we would have an all-night convenience store.

"But, let me put it this way. Which would you prefer? To go to California or Toronto to do your social work degree? If I can put away some money, you might just have the school of your choice. Mind you, that would mean no automobile upgrade at the local government housing parking lot this year. Even worse," I said, "some of the political appointees that cost us a quarter of a billion a year might have to give up something."

"You are really cruel to take away people's dignity for the sake of an all-night convenience store," she said.

I could see that Martha was getting exasperated by the conversation so I said, "If you really believe in the labour market and remuneration discrimination, then you and Duncan can do the dishes while your mother and I, as the working classes, take our leave from this tawdry pursuit."

Martha and I left the kids with the dishes and went to the den. She asked, "What did Paul tell you?"

"Actually, it sounds good. We can get Harry to set up our inheritance in a trust and then the principal can continue to earn and be recapitalized until we take money out. Even then the money we take out will be considered capital and untaxed."

"Why don't we set something like that up for Dunc and Katy?"

"A problem would arise because we are all Canadians. Therefore, the trust would be considered by CRA to be Canadian and any undistributed income in the trust would be taxed. There would be no advantage. In Harry's case, he is a non-Canadian setting up a trust for a Canadian and the trust is resident where it is registered and where the trustees are located. There were two good things I found out. The first is that trusts are not recorded anywhere so they are hard for the taxation people to find. That may become less of an advantage as the tax department has questions on the tax forms regarding trusts. It seems that by law they are not allowed to ask some of those kinds of questions if they don't concern your current income, but Paul tells me the law means nothing to the tax department."

"What we could do, Stew, is get my sister in the States to set up a trust for us using our money."

"No," I said, "that would cause her problems. In the U.S. tax system, she would be taxed on the amount she put into a non-philanthropic trust as a gift tax. In the U.S., when you try to give away money, you are taxed. As well, as the grantor of the trust, she might have the income of the trust assigned to her.

"The second item we talked about was that you can use trusts to shield your assets. You remember how concerned we were when that shyster our firm did business with threatened us with a law suit? As partners we were all liable for the debts of the partnership. Even if we turned the enterprise into a limited company, which would cost us some of our tax benefits, the directors of the company would be liable. However, what I am going to do is place my share of the family assets in a trust for you and the kids. That way if I am sued or the partnership is sued and we lose, the plaintiffs can't get our assets. I am going to recommend that all the partners do likewise."

"Good idea, Stew. Is the other case with that flake from

the entertainment business still alive?"

"I know what you're thinking," I said. "That case is barely alive, but if I undertook an asset protection trust now it would not protect us from anything instituted before the trust was formed. But, there is a wrinkle even to that rule. Although the transfer of the assets may be considered a fraudulent transfer in our courts, the Bahamian Courts would not listen to an appeal to attach the assets if they had been in the trust for more than two years."

"That's a full day's work for a Saturday," Martha said. "And here I thought you were just knocking a squash ball around in that remnant from the social dark ages."

"You'll be disgusted to learn that Angelo is going to meet me at the Toronto Racquet Club tomorrow to talk about tax havens," I said.

"Your choice?"

"No, his."

"When you see him, tell him to leave his cigars at home, wherever that might be, when he comes for dinner."

Martha was referring to Angelo's lifestyle. It was hard to know where he lived. He had become a tax exile. Officially his home was Ireland, although he hadn't been there permanently for some time. However, according to CRA's rules, if he no longer had a permanent residence, he was a resident of the last place he lived and was tax liable in that country, in his case, Ireland. Seeing as that was too advantageous for him, CRA decided to ignore that rule. He wasn't suffering though as there was an apartment in Toronto that a company kept for his use. With the apartment came a large Porsche car that was purchased by the company from a bankrupt real-estate agent. He spent his summers in the Mediterranean sailing on a 43-foot Hans Christian yacht.

The man had the use of the best of everything but owned nothing. He paid no income taxes,* yet had excellent health care that he purchased through private insurance. When I asked him about all this, he replied that he liked to buy everything up front from a private vendor. That way he knew exactly what he was getting. An example he described was police protection. In Oakville, where I reside, police protection is provided as part of the bundle of municipal services funded by my taxes. I have no recourse to the police except through a maze of complaint boards and municipal administrators. At his apartment, he has a private police force protecting the premises. His source of protection knows it can be fired at the first sign of sloth. If they foul up and his property is broken into, he can sue them. If my premises are broken into, I can't sue my protection agency, which is the municipal police. He pointed out to me that while government did not guarantee the services they provided, private vendors had to. It was then that my worries began — I realized that the Canadian government had promised me a comfortable retirement and health care in my old age but had not guaranteed it. The health care in particular was becoming a worry as one of my friends was on the waiting list for a heart operation and my father had waited six months for a knee replacement that still had not taken place.

As if reading my mind, Martha said, "Did you hear on the news that the government is putting more money into health care?"

---

* Angelo was subject to the most unavoidable of all taxes, consumption tax. Every purchase he made in most countries was subject to a sales tax of some form. Completely unavoidable.

"That's meaningless sweetheart. Twenty years ago the governments cut back on the number of places available in the medical schools. As a result there is a shortage of general practitioners, the first person you see in the health system. That clever move was designed to lower usage of the system. All it did was increase wait times and overwork the doctors. That combined with salary caps have encouraged some to leave. Two cardiologists from St. Michael's Hospital, who used to play at the squash club, just left for the States. If the drain continues, we won't have any members from St. Michael's Hospital in a couple of years."

"I think you should be more concerned about health care than the membership of that smelly jock, men's bastion. If you have a stroke or heart attack on the squash court, it won't help that you are two blocks from the St. Mike's. There won't be anyone there."

"You are being an alarmist," I said. "It is not as bleak as you say."

"Stewart, I am starting to worry about breast cancer and your prostate at the same time as health care is starting to be cut back. Our only hope here is to put away a nest egg in case one of us or the kids get really sick and we have to leave the country for treatment."

"Okay, okay. I'll get going on it."

CHAPTER 4

Travel Tips
FOR YOUR MONEY

On Sunday, I arrived at the squash club early for my 2:00 p.m. appointment with Angelo. There were a number of members in the sauna and on the courts sweating out the previous night's excesses while the steward routinely shielded them from phone calls. He would always ask the member if he was here before admitting it to the caller.

Angelo arrived punctually as he claimed, "Punctuality was the pride of princes." We began a game of eight-ball billiards and after the break I told Ang that I had looked into trusts for tax avoidance but I was now fascinated with the idea of tax havens.

"Wonderful things, trusts. I will probably set one up if I return to Canada."

"It wouldn't work for you," I said.

"Why not? I will be setting up the trust as a non-resident of Canada. If that won't work, I'll set one up under the immigrant's scheme and get a five-year shield for my assets and their earnings."

"Isn't that an abuse of the rules?"

"Stewart, it's what I call 'financial judo.' Judo is Japanese for 'the gentle way.' As a martial art, it involves taking the opponent's thrusts and strengths and using them against him while at the same time exploiting his weaknesses.

"The tax department attempts to collect as much money as possible for its political masters. As Colbert, the finance minister to one of the French kings, pointed out, good taxation consists of 'the plucking of the goose with the least amount of squawking.' However, it has been proven time and again that taxes are an impediment to economic activity. So, a line exists that the tax department has to balance on in order to extract as much as possible from the system without closing it down. Therefore, institutions have been created to allow the economic system to continue while funds are being drained out of the system. These are legitimate undertakings. The challenge that arises is in setting them up to work for the individual. All tax avoidance is based on using the government's rules for the individual's benefit rather than what these rules were designed for — the tax department's benefit.

"So what do you know about tax avoidance?" he asked me.

"I understand trusts but as for the rest of it, consider me a blank slate. Let's start from scratch," I said.

"Tax avoidance works with income sources you can

direct, such as investment, fee, and commission income. The operative idea is to separate the taxable individual from the source of income and redirect it. Usually the earnings are directed to a jurisdiction where they will incur no tax, in other words, a tax haven."

"What is a 'tax haven'?" I asked.

"A tax haven is a place where the taxes on a particular type of income are lower than what you would pay in your current jurisdiction. You take inheritance taxes for instance. For an American, Canada is a tax haven because there is no inheritance tax. So, if an American were to become a resident in Canada prior to dying, his death tax would be based on the increase in the value of his assets during his residency, not on their total value as in the U.S. Greece is a tax haven for some because it does not tax foreign-source income. This was a sop that was set up for the ship owners who derived all their income outside the country. Ireland is a tax haven for artists who can reside there without paying tax on their artistic earnings."

"Why would a country set up systems that give tax advantages? The country that does so is giving up revenue."

"Is it, Stew? You take Ireland. It has a very high value added tax, or VAT. When the high-earning artist comes to live in Ireland, he spends on the basis of his income and that is taxed at the time of expenditure. So, the Irish government has lost the income tax of this new resident but it has gained the consumption taxes of a resident who moved because of this tax law. Seems like good business to me. What you are seeing in the Irish situation is a deliberate tax haven as opposed to an accidental haven.

"Some tax havens, such as Bermuda and Switzerland, evolved, while others, like the Cayman Islands and the

Turks and Caicos Islands, were created. Evolutionary tax
havens occurred because the laws were created in order to
protect the individual's wealth. The Swiss, who are fierce
democrats, believe that you cannot have personal freedom
without providing security of property. Their legal system is
geared towards the protection of the individual's right to
own assets without the interference of government. Switzerland became a tax haven because Geneva was on the French
border. In 1792, when the French revolutionary mob was
relieving the plutocracy of their heads and their purses,
there was a flight of wealth to Switzerland. The Swiss discovered that this created an industry that was effortless,
non-polluting, and highly profitable. To encourage even
more flight capital to immigrate to Switzerland, they continuously sought new ways to protect capital from ravenous
governments. Therefore, tax evasion, which is a crime in
most countries, is not considered a crime in Switzerland.
When a foreign government asks for the bank records of a
depositor because of his criminal activity, the Swiss do not
have to provide the records if the activity being described
is tax evasion as this is not a crime in Switzerland. The
same applies in most tax haven juridictions.

"Another cornerstone of tax avoidance is secrecy. So,
unlike the popular myth attributing bank secrecy to the
need of anonymity by European Jews fleeing persecution,
the Swiss numbered bank account was in existence before
their needs arose. Swiss bank secrecy had arisen as an
adjunct to financial discretion. Because of their long established position in the tax avoidance industry, Switzerland
is the name that comes to most people's lips when they
think of hidden wealth. Because it is so well known, it is
also the most expensive. Whenever the police think that

there might have been fraud by government officials or money laundering, the first place they look is Switzerland because it is the name that they are most familiar with. It is therefore used today by the unsophisticated. Switzerland as a tax haven evolved.

"In the case of the Caymans, the British government decided at some point in time that it could no longer afford to pay the cost of supporting the islanders. When sugar was rare and expensive, the Caribbean Islands were a source of wealth to the British plantation owners. When the sugar beet was found to be a source of sugar and sugar cane began to be grown all over the world, sugar prices collapsed and the islands became liabilities rather than assets.

"At first, tourism was thought to be the answer to the islands' economic problems. However, the Jamaicans, when they became independent, had given tourism a black eye in the Caribbean. Although warned that their abuse of the tourists would soon lead to their flight, the Jamaicans refused to believe that there could be anywhere with similar beaches and climate. Then they saw their tourist industry move to Mexico. All the islands suffered and the British had to find a new industry for their remaining colonies in the West Indies. They needed only to look offshore to the islands in the English Channel to find it. Both Guernsey and Jersey, although lacking in any kind of natural industry, were prospering by offering tax haven opportunities to the world. It was a simple leap of mind to consider the Cayman Islands as the world's next tax haven. There was a large market located just to the north of the Caymans — the U.S. — which was ready and waiting for this kind of entity, and so a tax haven was born. The Cayman islanders wanted their operation to be the best in the world and so they set up their banking and corporate laws to make their islands a financial fortress. As a result, the Cayman Islands today have $624 billion U.S. under administration, making them the third largest financial centre in the world, after New York and Tokyo."

"Wow, what a success story," I said. "As a kid, I can remember watching television ads for tourism in the Caymans. In recent years, I've seen none. The islanders obviously no longer want sweaty, oily bodies on their beaches. The Caymans must have the best system in the world."

"No, the Turks and Caicos Islands are probably the toughest jurisdiction to penetrate today. You see, when Canada turned down those islands' request to become the 11th province, fearing that they might become the financial drain on Canada that they were for Britain, the islanders tried tourism. That didn't provide prosperity so they hired the people who set up the Caymans as a tax haven to do the same for them. The next thing you knew, there were branches of Barclays and the Bank of Nova Scotia on the islands and various Canadian and U.S. stockbrokers were opening offices. The place is booming and there are very few oil-soaked tourists sweating it out on their beaches. It is no longer rich North Americans that are wanted: it is their money."

"Where will it end?"

"When they run out of islands, Stew. Even poor little Nevis is now a tax haven. It is so new that the banks have to chase the chickens out of their offices."

"Why don't the countries that are losing tax revenues close down the tax havens?" I asked.

"I'm sure they would like to, but there is a problem. Many of the tax havens are protectorates of major European countries. If the U.S. or Canadian governments were to go after Curaçao, for example, the Dutch government would intervene. The same holds for the Caymans as they are a British protectorate.

"As well there is the problem of the inconvenience that would be caused to Canada's political and economic elites. For example Paul Martin, the former Prime Minister of Canada, ran his steamship companies through first Bermuda and then the Barbados. If those tax havens were to be closed down, he like many Canadian first families would find themselves paying income tax in Canada. But, with these two points — the concept of a deliberate tax haven and the existence of a major power as protector — you have addressed the two most important questions regarding the choice of a tax haven."

"I can understand the protectorate concept but what is so important about the deliberate tax haven versus the accidental?"

"Let's take the Bahamas as an example of an accidental tax haven. It has been used for tax avoidance because of its British-based bank secrecy rules and trust laws. The problem that arose was that prior to the 1986 changes in their banking laws, if an employee were to provide the IRS or CRA with your financial data there were no penalties. Now, like all of the deliberate tax havens, they have laws guarding corporate and bank secrecy that, if broken, lead to penalties.

"The Bahamas has another interesting aspect. When you look at the Bahamian economy, you will observe that less than 25 percent of the gross domestic product comes from tax avoidance services, while in excess of 70 percent comes from tourism. A large majority of those tourists come from nearby Florida. If the U.S. government wanted access to Bahamian financial records, they could easily use the threat of a required, expensive travel visa, thus choking off their tourist industry. The Bahamians would have to choose between the small amount of tax avoidance income and the large tourist business. I'm sure that tourism would be the winner."

"That sounds disgusting," I said. "I doubt that any developed country, like the U.S., would resort to strong-arm tactics, such as blackmail or extortion, to achieve its ends. I'll bet it has never been done."

"Sorry to be the bearer of bad tidings, Stew, but the Americans already did just that to Bermuda. When they wanted financial records of U.S. citizens with assets in Bermuda, they threatened the Bermudians with an impediment to their reinsurance market, which was more substantial than the tax avoidance business, and got what they wanted."

"Why didn't the Bermudians turn to the British to help them?"

"Because Bermuda, like the Bahamas, is an independent country and not a British protectorate."

"I understand," I said. "If you use a country that is a deliberate and dedicated tax haven, you are dealing with a place where the tax business is sacrosanct."

"As well, you are in an environment where the laws and structures are designed to protect the individual from the tax collectors."

While I was engrossed in listening to Angelo, I neglected to notice that he had just about cleaned off the billiard table. It was beginning to look like I was going to get stuck for the drinks yet again. I didn't mind. I had just received a priceless lesson regarding tax havens. I now knew that the term "tax haven" applied to any place with better tax rates than you were currently being subjected to. As well, there were characteristics of tax havens that made some more desirable than others. First and foremost, they had to be deliberate rather than accidental, and they had to have a protector. Not bad for the cost of a jug of beer. I looked down my cue at the three ball and said, "So, that's all I need to know about tax havens?"

"No, those are the most important points, but you should be aware of some other points as well. For example, the legal system. You should choose a tax haven that uses British common law so that you are familiar with the legal framework.

"Also, you should be cautious about certain places, such as Barbados, that have a tax treaty with the U.S. or Canada. Tax treaties allow for the sharing of tax and financial information. What good would it do you to pursue financial secrecy only to have it stripped away by a tax treaty? But then, there are times when you may want to use a country that has a treaty. That usually occurs if you want to pursue a commercial or business use of tax havens.

"And then there is the question of currency controls. You don't want to deal in any place you can get your money into but not out of.

"Speaking of money, it makes life much simpler if the jurisdiction you are dealing in uses the U.S. dollar. That way you avoid exchange costs every time you move funds and there is no threat of devaluation.

"Location matters as well. You don't want to be using a tax haven located in a place like Cyprus, which is seven time zones away from where you are. It means that you have to get up in the middle of the night to have a phone conversation with the administrators.

"Even political stability matters, although it is of minor importance because few people who use tax havens have their assets in the same location as their structure's domicile."

I watched the eight ball slide effortlessly into the side pocket as Angelo made a perfect cross-table bank shot. It was now payback time and I had the steward bring us a pitcher of shandy.

"There seems to be a lot to know," I said. "There are an immense number of factors to consider when choosing which tax haven to use."

"No, it's mostly just common sense. When looking at a tax haven, what you are seeking is a place with security, stability, and safety. You should apply these three S's to any financial undertaking."

I then remembered having read in the newspaper about mutual legal assistance treaties and the tax havens. I asked Angelo, "What are these mutual legal assistance treaties I've been hearing about?"

"Those are part of the desperate measures the high tax jurisdictions are taking to try to avoid the financial bleeding they are experiencing. In 1999, the Germans noticed there was 485 billion Deutschmarks missing from their economy. Originally, they had cracked down on banks in Luxembourg to try and force the tax rebels to repatriate their money. But, instead of it coming home, it went to the tax havens. When the Germans and other EU countries approached the tax havens and asked to see the books of people with German addresses to pursue them for tax evasion, they were told that these people had not com-

mitted a crime in the country of the haven so their financial records could not be opened. You see, Stewart, the tax
havens will gladly open the books of a person who is
charged with a crime, but it has to be an act that is recognized as a crime in the country of the haven. In this case,
how could you have the crime of tax evasion in a jurisdiction where the individual had no personal income taxes?

"The answer was the mutual legal assistance treaties,
which say that what is a crime in my country is a crime in
yours and vice versa."

"How could the countries with high taxes force the
havens to agree to this?" I asked.

"The U.S. and the EU ganged up on the small havens
and threatened to cut off their access to banking and other
international services. In other words, banks located in the
tax havens would not be able to clear cheques, money
orders, or letters of credit through banks in the U.S. or EU.
Some of the havens have signed these with the attitude that
their business is tax avoidance and hence these treaties are
not a threat. Others have recognized the treaties as the thin
edge of the wedge of extraterritorial interference and have
balked. Some of the governments that signed these were
thrown out of office in subsequent elections."

"What do you think of the treaties, Angelo?"

"As you know, some tax havens depend on financial
services for as much as 80 percent of their GDP. I doubt
that they are going to see this taken away from them. So,
one could say it's the first shot across the bow. Also, as long
as you scrupulously obey the law and avoid rather than
evade taxes, the mutual legal assistance treaties should be
of no concern. In some places like the Isle of Man, the
banks no longer offer chequing facilities in U.S. dollars

because of the clearing restrictions through U.S. banks. The unintended consequences are that the U.S. clearing banks have lost a portion of their business to Euro and Pound banks and there is less visibility to U.S. authorities on the movements of funds internationally. But there are other problems of unintended consequences.

"As you have learned, Stew, some of the tax havens have legislated bank and corporate secrecy. Included with that are penalties for attempting to overcome that secrecy. So, you could have a tax man writing a letter in the U.S. to a tax haven asking about a bank account on which he is not a signing authority. This would clearly break the laws of the tax haven and they could ask for the extradition of that person to the haven for prosecution."

We had talked about everything but costs. "Do the costs vary from one jurisdiction to another?"

"As you would expect, the locations that have been around for a long time and have the greatest prestige and marketplace recognition are most expensive. Therefore, Switzerland is probably the most expensive location, whereas the most recent havens, such as the Turks and Caicos Islands, are the cheapest."

"I now understand what a tax haven is. Now tell me how it works."

"Okay, Stewart, but it will cost you another game. What will it be — snooker or eight ball again?"

I chose snooker as I wasn't getting into form with eight ball, and I figured I could stick him for the beer if we played a different game.

CHAPTER 5

The Birth of the
"IMPERIAL BOND TRUST AND FORAGING COMPANY LIMITED"

"Angelo, I now know what a tax haven is. What I don't know is how to make it work for me."

"As I mentioned earlier, the tax haven can only be used with income you can direct, such as investment, commission, and sales earnings, or with assets. It is impossible for a wage earner to use these vehicles except under very special circumstances.

"To take the simplest example, let's say you have accumulated $200,000 in investments. Every year you make 10 percent on your money so you bring in $20,000 on the investment. If you live in Ontario, Canada, you can consider those earnings as on the margin of your income and the most highly taxed at about 50 percent. So, you will give

$10,000 to the provincial and federal governments and be left with $10,000."

"That pretty well explains the low national savings rate the economists are complaining about," I said.

"It certainly explains the reluctance of people to save; it's just not worth their while on an after-tax basis. But, let's look at that same $200,000 invested at 10 percent by a company that is resident in the Turks and Caicos Islands. It would earn $20,000 in a year and pay no income or corporate tax of any kind. Who is better off? You investing from Canada, or the offshore company investing from the islands?"

"Obviously, the offshore company," I said. "But there must be some costs involved."

"There is the original incorporation fee of about $2,000 and the annual fees of about $2,000."

"I can see the whole picture now. All I have to do is incorporate a company in the Turks and Caicos Islands and place all my capital with the company and have it earn tax-free investment income."

"Slow down, Stew. You've got the basic idea, but so do the Canada Customs and Revenue Agency and the U.S. Internal Revenue Service. If the taxation authorities allowed you to just place your investments outside of their jurisdiction with no return to them, then one of two things would happen. The ability of politicians to buy votes with your money would end or they would bankrupt the country. Neither of these is an acceptable outcome to the 'men of the trough,' and so the tax arm has been extended. The form of the extension is the same the world over. The tax chasers say if you control a private, passive corporation, all of the income of that corporation is in fact yours and taxable in your hands."

"That's a new term," I said. "What do you mean by a

'passive' corporation?"

"It is a company that has no traditional production or service-type activities. To be an active company and hence out of the scrutiny of the taxers, it must have five full-time employees and it must either provide a service other than portfolio management or produce a product. If you control a company that does not meet those requirements, then the company is regarded as a tax-avoidance vehicle and you are subject to tax on its earnings."

"There is an easy way out of that," I said. "Don't control the corporation."

"Exactly. When you set up the corporation in the tax haven, you do not take any of the common shares nor do you allow yourself to be appointed as a director or an officer. In other words, you cannot be a director, the president, the secretary, or the treasurer of the company. Because you do not have any common shares, you cannot be accused of being in control of the company."

"How do I maintain control?" I asked. "Do I have options or warrants to get common stock?"

"No. If you did, then CRA would say that you have the ability to gain control of the company, therefore, you do in fact control it and the earnings are yours for tax purposes. The American tax authorities would look at the corporation's share holdings to determine if it was, by their definition, a 'Personal Holding Company.' If so, they would take the earnings, on a pro rata basis, and tax them as your personal earnings."

"So what you are telling me, Ang, is that I have to set up a company in which I have no shares and no control position. If I did that, how would I direct the activities of the company? The company could abscond with my assets, make stupid decisions, and enrich the officers. How could I prevent any of this?"

"In the first instance, you have to remember that this company is being administered in a jurisdiction that is in the business of providing tax avoidance. Neither the organization nor the government of that jurisdiction want to do anything that might harm their reputation as a place where your money can go and work for you. The country's economy is based on the fees and charges you incur. In the financial industry, reputation is everything. There was an instance of malfeasance in one of the jurisdictions, but rather than have the matter reach the courts with the subsequent publicity, the government paid off the investors and closed down the administrator.

"As well, the organizations that provide these tax-haven vehicles have engineered structures that give the initial investor the ability to move the company to another administrator if there is malfeasance.

"The second point to consider is that you want the administration of the assets in the company, not the company itself. I have always described this process of tax avoidance for investment income as possession versus ownership. If you were to walk out of here with a kilogram of cocaine in your pocket and were stopped by the police, they would charge you with possession of narcotics not ownership. You could very easily be transporting the drugs for someone else, but the important point is that they are in your possession. As the old saying goes, possession is nine-tenths of the law. However, in the taxation industry, ownership takes precedence over possession for many considerations. In my case, I possess $250,000 of Pfizer debentures. They are registered in the name of 'Barolo

Corporation' of the Turks and Caicos Islands. Whose debentures are they?"

"The certificates are the property of Barolo," I said. "Because they are registered in the company's name."

"They certainly are, but Barolo can't sell or pledge them because I have them in my safety deposit box in Miami."

"I get it. When Pfizer gives the U.S. government the list of investors receiving interest, then Barolo's name, and not yours, will be one of the names on the list. If it was in your name, then either the U.S. or Canadian government would come chasing you for tax on the interest. But this way, the responsible taxing authority is the country where the company resides and they don't charge tax. Great idea. But isn't there withholding tax on the interest?"

"Fortunately, the governments have dug their own graves on that issue. When they discovered deficit financing as a way to defer taxation on the masses, they had to have a source of borrowing. Investors would buy their bonds only if they got the interest tax free. Corporations then demanded the same benefits to be able to compete in the loan markets. If, in the U.S., you or your broker files a W-8 form showing that the purchaser is a foreigner investing for portfolio purposes, when a debenture or bond is purchased, you will pay no withholding tax on the interest. So, the interest arrives in the Turks and Caicos tax free and is not liable for tax there. In Canada, if a bond or debenture was issued by a publicly listed corporation with a maturity of more than five years or was issued by the federal or a provincial government, the interest can be received by a foreign holder tax free."

"That means tax-free interest," I said. "I love it because I have always believed that once you paid tax on earned income it was yours to do with as you pleased and there should be no penalty for savings. Our boys and girls in government wouldn't charge me a 50 percent penalty if I went out and bought a Rolls-Royce with the $200,000. So they obviously want me to spend rather than save. Once I put the money away in a tax haven the decision to spend or save becomes tax neutral. How absolutely sensible.

"Also," I said, "the asset is in my possession but the title lies in somebody else's name so I have shifted the tax liability. By maintaining possession, I protect the asset. It is beautiful in its simplicity. But, what if I actually want to use the asset either to sell or pledge for a loan? Even worse, perhaps my tax shelter falls apart. How would I ever negotiate the debenture?"

"No problem, Stew. If you actually want to keep the certificate in your possession, you could ask the local broker to obtain the certificate registered in the corporation's name and provide you with the certificate and a power of attorney to negotiate it."

"Do you keep all of Barolo's certificates?" I inquired.

"No, that really is unnecessary. You haven't seen the full structure, Stew. When Barolo was incorporated, it opened a stock trading account.

"The stock trading account was with a broker in the haven. The reason for using a foreign broker is that if Canada Revenue Agency or the Internal Revenue Service came snooping around they wouldn't be able to pressure the broker into releasing any information. When you deal with a financial institution in the same jurisdiction as your potential tax liability, you are taking a gamble. The government can bring unbearable pressure on a broker or bank that will eventually cause them to disregard their need to protect yours or anybody's confidentiality. They will even act in disregard of the law of the land if asked to by the tax collectors."

"Aren't you going a bit far, Ang?" I asked.

"In the past, two Canadian banks were pressured by CRA. The banks caved in and provided information on accounts in Bermuda and the Bahamas. In doing so, they broke the law of the land in Bermuda and Bahamas, which have always insisted that their banks observe bank secrecy.

"In 1995, CRA asked banks in foreign jurisdictions to provide interest receipts known as T-5's for all their Canadian clients banking in foreign branches. For many of the branches in foreign countries, this would violate bank secrecy rules and be an extraterritorial extension of Canadian law, sort of like the Helms-Burton Bill passed by the U.S. Congress punishing non-U.S. residents for using assets stolen by the Cubans. The Canadian government complains about the extraterritorial efforts of those U.S. bullies, but fails to recognize that it is doing exactly the same bullying.

"The other problem created for Canadian banks by the government's insatiable lust for money is that customers are fleeing to banks of other nationalities to avoid having their business affairs exposed to Canada Revenue Agency, thus costing the Canadian banks business."

"Can't anything be done to restrict the operations of the tax gunslingers?* Are the courts useless?" I asked.

---

* If you read the *Income Tax Act*, you will find that there are rules that must be obeyed by the tax collectors and taxpayers. If the taxpayer breaks the rules, there are penalties. If the tax collector breaks his rules, there are no penalties. An example is audits, which, according to the rules, can only be used to determine if a taxpayer has paid his obligatory tax. These are now used by the collections branch to determine from third parties if someone being pursued has income or assets. Complaints to the government have, so far, fallen on deaf ears.

"The way the system works is that the government will threaten you with all sorts of laws that would never stand the smell test of being in violation of your civil liberties and natural justice. If you should stand firm, they will probably back away, especially if you are a corporation or other entity with deep pockets. If you do go to court, you can't count on winning, even with an ironclad case, because you have to bear in mind where the judges come from. They are old party hacks with law degrees."

"How do the civil libertarian groups feel about the violation of people's rights by the tax extortionists?" I asked. "Won't they do something?"

"They are so in awe of the need to provide equal opportunity to black, lesbian, paraplegic single parents, that they don't have time for the rights of the masses.

"However, when you are dealing with a foreign broker, it need not supply any information to Canadian authorities and may be prohibited from doing so by the local laws. Therefore, I looked for a foreign broker to handle Barolo's account. When the account was established, I had myself appointed as the portfolio manager."

"How does a corporation open a stock account?" I inquired.

"There are a number of simple steps. The first is that the board of directors passes a resolution to open an account with a named individual to be the portfolio manager. Then a copy of the articles of incorporation, a copy of the board resolution, identification of the portfolio manager, and confirmation of the directors' signatures is sent to the broker. In most cases, the broker will only open a 'cash' account that precludes the corporation from margin or options trading. However, that is hardly an imposition because when an account can earn tax-free interest, why take the risk of investing in anything other than interest-bearing instruments."

"Angelo, risk is commensurate with reward; the more risk you take, the greater the reward. Why not use some of the more exotic investment choices?"

"You are right that reward increases with risk, but look at it from the other perspective. Risk increases exponentially with reward. If it were a straight-line equation, I would have fewer qualms, but that is a whole other issue. Therefore, the reluctance of the investment firms to offer margin accounts to offshore corporations does not strike me as a great impediment to the accumulation of wealth.

"In Barolo's situation, I had the company open an account with a local stockbroker (located in the tax haven) with myself as the portfolio manager. I then directed the broker as to which investments to purchase and sell. Any bonds that are held by the broker have their interest paid to the active account."

"Aren't you worried about the security of the local broker? What if he absconds with your funds or goes broke?" I asked.

"Ah, here is the trick. The local broker has an account with a major broker of my choice. In this case, Merrill Lynch. That is the real or active account. The corporation has a letter from Merrill stating that the funds must either be directed by me and my agent or they must flow into the Merrill account. There is no way that the funds can flow back to the local broker.

"You could also have the local broker open an online account and then provide the investor with the password. You could then change the password so that you would be the only one to have access to the account."

"Why not have the corporation open the account with Merrill directly, Ang?" I suggested.

"That is an interesting story. In days of old, that is exactly how it was done and there are many accounts around the world belonging to small offshore corporations. However, in recent years, the 'know your client rule' of the stock-brokerage industry has been re-worded by the taxers and is now the 'know your client intimately rule.' The old rule was set in place to determine the suitability of investments for the type of client. In other words, you didn't want a broker buying the latest dot com security for an 80-year-old widow, nor did you want to see a young bachelor holding a portfolio full of guaranteed investment certificates. To know if the investment was suitable for the client, you had to know the client's risk profile. Now, to appease the taxers, the brokerages have changed the emphasis of the know your client rule to be able to guarantee that the client isn't some form of tax avoider. So, if a corporation shows up as the client, the broker handling the account has to assure the firm's compliance department that this company would not offend the sensibilities of the tax department."

"This is beginning to sound goofy," I said. "So why does the local broker open the account with Merrill?"

"There is an established protocol that brokers can open accounts with other brokers with no scrutiny. If a local Cleveland, Ohio, broker wants to trade a Toronto Stock Exchange (TSE) listed security on behalf of a client, he can't. The way around it is for him to open an account with a TSE broker and let the Toronto broker execute the trade. So the way it works now, the offshore corporation opens an account with one of the haven brokers and that broker opens an account with a major worldwide brokerage. Also, as I mentioned before, there is a letter restricting the flow of funds back to the local broker. When the client wants to place an order, he calls the haven broker, who then executes the order at the major brokerage. The wonderful part is that the assets are domiciled in some nice safe country like England or the U.S.

"Also, there are still jurisdictions that will open an account directly for an International Business Corporation (IBC). Once the company is established the directors open an account in the Isle of Man, Jersey or some other haven. Clean and simple."

"If money or assets can't flow back to the local broker, how do you get your hands on the money?" I asked.

"My case is special because I'm a resident of a tax-benign country. With my structure, the funds are directed by the corporation owning the brokerage account to a bank account in my name in the channel islands where I can access it. Most people who set up an offshore structure only want to save money offshore and only begin to take money out when they retire.

"For the long-term investor, a class of participants who have special privileges is included in the incorporation. These privileges allow them to acccss the funds at any time, but this usually occurs and is used after retirement. If I was resident in North America, I would be uncomfortable with having a signing authority on a foreign account. In the U.S., taxpayers have to reveal if they have signing authority on a foreign account. In Canada, if you have more than $100,000 in a foreign bank account in your name, it has to be revealed on the tax forms. As you could have guessed, there is more disclosure now being demanded in the offshore arena. The reason being that since the tax havens have become accessible to the middle class and not just the wealthy, the taxers have pressured the banks for more information. Now when a corporation opens a bank account in a tax haven, there is the question 'who is the beneficial owner of the corporation' in the account-opening documents."

"Isn't that dangerous?" I asked.

"Yes and no. The banks are asking this question because of the governments' new found interest in money laundering. The EU and North American governments have told the masses that it benefits the people if the government knows where each dollar is going. This, of course, is false. The greatest benefit occurs when governments grant an amnesty on hidden funds, which then come out into the open where their investment can generate tax revenue. The desire to trace funds is to try to hobble the tax avoiders. The banks that know you are in the legal pursuit of tax avoiding are therefore not going to casually give your name as an account holder to the taxers. But the banks want to cover themselves just in case a Russian mafioso or Colombian drug dealer manages to open an account.

"There is the smell of hypocrisy here as governments are not so concerned about where money comes from when they are taxing. The important aspect of whether or not the mafioso or drug baron has beneficial ownership of a tax shelter is to be able to tax it. The Canadian government wasn't too proud to live off the avails of Mrs. MacDonald's Vancouver brothel in the 1950s, and I am sure there are a fair share of criminals paying their taxes. That's why tax records are secret.

"If you are willing to live with the fact that the bank knows who the beneficial owner of an offshore corporation is when you have gone to the trouble of distancing yourself from the ownership, then use a brokerage account with a haven broker connected to an account with a major worldwide broker. If you are still concerned, then insure your offshore capital."

"Who would possibly insure my capital in a tax haven?" I asked.

"Well, how about Lloyd's of London? The agent I know of is Cooper Gay in London and they will insure your capital for 20 basis points."

"Well that seems incredibly cheap. From the rates, I would surmise that the loss level must be quite low."

"It is so low that, for large amounts, Cooper Gay will reduce their rates to 15 basis points."

I was so excited by what Angelo was telling me that I was unfazed as I watched him sink the pink ball followed by the black to give me a thorough beating at snooker.

"I'll order another shandy," I said, "if you tell me how you go about getting an offshore corporation established."

CHAPTER 6

Offshore with
THE SHARKS

. . . .

"There is very little difference between the establishing of a corporation on the basis of jurisdiction or location. The proper documents have to be filed with the government body responsible for the registration of corporations. The individuals who do this tawdry job are often lawyers, but in some jurisdictions it is the responsibility of notaries. How would you handle it in Canada?" Angelo asked.

"One of two ways. Either I would fill out all the documents myself and take them to the Department of Commercial and Corporate Affairs or I would hire a lawyer to file the documents for me."

"The same is true in the offshore arena. The major difference is, with the offshore, you do not know with whom to file the papers, nor do you know how to do it. So, the locals make it easy for you.

"The easiest way in Curaçao is to speak to one of the many trust companies involved in the business. In the case of the Caymans, the same sort of institutions exist. In the Turks and Caicos, there are both lawyers and corporation vendors that are willing to provide you with a company with all your specifications for a fee. Also, you may have seen advertisements in financial periodicals offering 'off the shelf' corporations. The options are numerous but there are some caveats.

"As John Ruskin said, 'there is nothing that someone cannot make a little poorer and sell a little cheaper.' In the offshore-corporations business, like every other market, there are people who take advantage of the first-time buyer's ignorance. A first-time buyer is not likely to know that his offshore company will require directors, a bank or brokerage account, registered office and an administrator. Some of the postal vendors neglect to advertise with their very low prices that all the other necessities to make the vehicle operative have to be bought as separate items."

"The obvious answer to that," I said, "is to be sure that you are comparing apples to apples. You can bet that, as a first-time buyer, I will do my research first."

"That may not be sufficient, Stew. There are some people selling offshore companies who have no idea how these vehicles will be used. In one instance, an acquaintance approached me and asked if the company he had bought through a newspaper ad could be used for tax avoidance. My friend had been sent the shares and he and his wife were designated as directors. The result was that they were well-documented controlling shareholders, and so the company was useless to them.

"The first action to take is to determine what your needs are and then find the best vendor. In your case, Stewart, I would say that your needs are a corporation with the ability to run an investment account. If you were to follow in my footsteps, you would open a corporation in the Turks and Caicos Islands through one of the many agents that handle this business.* The agent who set up my structure uses a company administrator run by Canadian chartered accountants residing in those islands."

"What is so special about that?" I asked.

"They are aware of the tax laws of Canada and keep up with the ongoing changes."

"What will taxers do to stop this, Ang?"

"The Canadian government has new offshore reporting rules for Canadian taxpayers. What these rules say is that if you own 10 percent or more of a class of shares of a foreign corporation, then that company is said to be a foreign affiliate of yours and you have to provide financial statements for the company.

"These new rules don't make much sense to me. In fact, CRA has a rule known as section 231.6 of the *Income Tax Act* that allows the minister of finance to demand foreign-based information documents. This section of the act has proven to be particularly useless with respect to tax havens that refuse to answer impertinent questions. In the same vein, the proposed legislation would require the reporting of offshore investments that at any time exceeded $100,000 in value. This, as well, seems bizarre.

---

* One such company is Liberty Consulting, P.O. Box 378, Providenciales, Turks & Caicos Islands, British West Indies.

"Suppose you bought $90,000 worth of Citicorp Bank stock on the New York Stock Exchange. If, during inter-day trading, the shares climbed past $100,000 in value and then dropped back before the close of trading to a value of less than $100,000 for the balance of the year, you would have to report the event to CRA. If you didn't see that one trade and failed to note and report the event to CRA you would be subject to $12,000 in fines. As well seeing as Canadians are required to report all their worldwide income, any income from $100,000 or more of assets would have been reported. So if a taxpayer answers yes to this question his tax bill does not go up. If he answers no to the question his tax bill doesn't change. The question is irrelevant."

"Well then why the question regarding $100,000 in for-eign holdings?" I inquired.

"No one seems to know," Angelo responded.

"On second thought, maybe I would be better off establishing a trust," I said.

"They are trying to stop the use of trusts as well. If you provide assets to a trust, you are required to report a myriad of information on that trust. The information that you are required to provide to CRA consists of the name of the trust, trustees, beneficiaries, location, and protector. As well, they are seeking information regarding the indebted-ness of the beneficiaries to the trust and a complete history of the trust. Of course, much of that information is in the hands of the trustees and, if they were asked, they would tell the Canadian tax authorities to mind their own busi-ness and stop trying to impose their laws extraterritorially."

"What would you do?" I asked. "Would you go the trust or the corporate route?"

"It depends on your objectives, but I usually advise individuals to use the corporate structures as they are cheaper and more flexible than trusts. If the new reporting rules are bothering you, don't let them. I have spoken to accountants and lawyers who tell me that, even with the sketchy information supplied by the government, they have managed to engineer new vehicles to overcome the speed bumps that the taxers are putting in the way of financial security and confidentiality. After all, you have to remember that the individuals who are trying to stop people from securing their old age are of the intelligence of the labour leader who recommended to the premier of a province that was borrowing $8 billion per year to pay its welfare bills, that the province should renege on its debts."

"Hey, that's not a bad idea. The province wouldn't have to pay back the principal or interest," I said.

"That's true, Stewart, but if you renege on your debts you can't borrow any more money and the province had to borrow to pay its expenses. By and large, the governments are getting that quality of advice. The advisors to our team are much smarter."

"What new structures have the financial engineers come up with?"

"They involve the use of trusts in conjunction with corporations and more elegant share structures in combination with options to overcome the new reporting rules. Also, remember that much of the information that the taxers want rests with foreign jurisdictions that are not going to give it up."

"Well, why is the government going through this exercise?" I asked.

"There are two answers. The first is that as long as they

continue to propose but don't enact new rules, people, not knowing what restrictions will prevail, will be reluctant to move their assets to safety. The other is that the new rules only provide the basis for CRA to begin an investigation of a taxpayer. If the information asked for is provided, it does not necessarily form the foundation of an assessment for tax purposes. The information being sought is for the purpose of a fishing expedition. It is not for the reporting of income for tax purposes and, therefore, probably beyond the scope of the *Income Tax Act*. But, the accumulation of information by governments is always dangerous. Remember that in the 1930s in Germany, at first the Nazis only asked for the German Jews to register with the government. Then, they used that information to murder them.

"There are other problems for the taxers. Any new rules to be effective are probably going to be a violation of your constitutional rights and natural justice. This will cause two things. It will cause the re-engineering of the tax-avoidance structures by the accountants and lawyers. It will also cause a breakdown in respect for the laws once people determine they are unjust. It is the second point that worries the tax authorities the most, as income tax is a self-assessing system with very low collection costs in North America. In countries where the system has been seen to be abusive, it is disregarded. Take Greece, for example. Many years ago taxpayers saw that their tax dollars were going into the politicians' pockets directly. They weren't even stopping to be rinsed through the systems of patronage and pork barrelling. So, the Greeks stopped paying income tax to the extent that the state collects less than 25 percent of the taxes due and the single largest contributor to the Greek treasury is the European Union and its handouts. In countries where you see a reliance on consumption taxes, such as 'value added' and 'sales' taxes, you can be sure that the income tax system has run into problems."

"Isn't there anything that the government can do to stop citizens from hiding their assets?" I asked.

"Sure there is. Just drop tax rates."

CHAPTER 7

A Guide to
OUTSIDER TRADING

Later in the week I was in the locker room at the squash club putting away my gear when one of the younger members who was a stockbroker came over.

"Wasn't that the fellow described in *Take Your Money and Run!* I saw you with on Sunday?" he asked.

"Yes, it was, David. Do you know him?"

"No, but I know of him. He has been my major source of business over the past three years. I now have about 120 accounts that are tax-avoidance structures. After reading that book, I found a company called 'Liberty Consulting of the Turks & Caicos' in the Toronto phonebook, which did company formations all over the globe. I described to them how their clients could work with a foreign broker to set up brokerage accounts with my firm in Toronto. I have an ironclad structure that provides local clients with a high degree of security. The beneficiaries of the offshore structures who reside here can walk past our offices every day and know that their assets are sitting securely in our vaults."

"I think I know what you are talking about," I said. "Angelo told me that when dealing with the offshore, you should always deal with a foreign broker so as to remove the threat of a penetration of confidentiality by the domestic tax authorities. But to have that foreign broker deal with somebody substantial. I gather that is your firm."

"Angelo is right but old-fashioned. In his day, after the company was formed, money was moved into it from Canada with little concern. Now, that is not as easy. Let me describe how things are done today.

"Let's say you wanted to set up a tax-deferral structure. Where is your favourite tax haven?" David asked.

"Well, I don't know. I'll choose the Turks and Caicos because they have a good beach."

"What I would do is have an international business corporation set up for you at a cost of U.S.$2,000. In the company, all the common shares would be owned by the corporation's agents in the Turks. The agent, as a result of owning the shares, would be able to appoint the company's board of directors. At incorporation, a special class of 'B' shares would be created. These have no value but the holder of any B share has the right to dismiss the board of directors. Interestingly, this B share has a total issue of 20 shares and one of the shares goes to a person of your choice. I usually call this person a golden shareholder.

"The company opens a brokerage account with a local broker and the broker is instructed to open a segregated account with my firm. There you have it. An International Business Corporation (IBC) now exists and has the ability to invest on the behalf of some poor overtaxed North American."

"There are some things I don't understand," I said. "What about that golden share, if the company were being opened for me would I get that?"

"No. That share allows the holder to dismiss the company's board of directors. This is similar to the way that the protector of a trust has the ability to move the trust. The function of the share would be that if the company's administrators were not attending to your needs properly, you would have the holder of the share dismiss the board. At that point, a new administrator for the company could be found."

"Why don't I hold that share, David?"

"My feeling is that if you controlled the IBC's stock account and had the golden share, CRA could make a case that you controlled the company."

"But, doesn't the golden shareholder control the company?"

"No. Look at what the rule says, 'If an individual has the ability to appoint the majority of the board of a company, he controls the company.' That is not the same as being able to dismiss the board.

"The B share just formalizes what was an older feature of IBC structures whereby the person forming the company would be given an undated letter of resignation of the board of directors of the company. What that did was take the company out of the control of the current agent and allow the appointment of a new administrator or agent for the company if the client was dissatisfied."

"Why the two different approaches, David?" I asked.

"If the board is changed during the life of the company, the client may not have an effective letter of resignation if the named directors are not current. This could occur if one of the directors named is no longer an employee of the agent. As well, some of the havens allow companies to be directors of companies, which further clouds the effectiveness of the letter of resignation "

"Couldn't all of this be eliminated by issuing bearer shares to the client?" I inquired. "As the only shareholder with all the bearer shares, the investor would have complete control of the company."

"Stew, the taxing authorities would say that if you possessed the bearer shares, you were in control of the company. If you were questioned on this and lied, you would be in trouble. In any case, bearer securities are out of favour. The governments want every financial instrument registered so that they can keep track of who owns what. Even the most ubiquitous of bearer instruments, money, is being suppressed. In the old days, you would hear the cry 'cash is king,' but no longer. See what happens if you walk into your bank with a couple thousand dollars in cash to deposit. If you are a retail client, you will fill out an enormous form. If you are a business client, not only will you be required to do the paperwork but you will also have to pay a fee to deposit cash. By law you have to accept a dollar as a medium of exchange and to settle debts, but you can't use it. So, if bearer money is no longer acceptable, just think of what going up the ladder of financial instruments will do for you."

"So, for 2,000 bucks, I could have a corporation in a tax haven with a stock account to hold my investments. I would be free from seizure and able to defer the taxes indefinitely. That sounds wonderful," I said.

"Not so fast, Stew. Where are you going to get the money to fund it?"

"I'll just send a cheque or wire transfer."

"Well, let's say you sent a cheque or wire for $200,000. Your tax profile in the second year would change. CRA would ask, 'Where are the investment earnings that you reported on that $200,000 you had?' If you said that you lent it to an offshore corporation, CRA would impose an interest rate on that loan, and attribute the interest income to you.

"If, on the other hand, you said that you gave it as a gift to the company, CRA would declare any earnings on that gift as yours. According to the government, there are acceptable gifts and unacceptable. Any gift that is to your benefit is unacceptable.

"You now know how the tax authorities are fighting the offshore. It is through the stopping of funds flowing into the structures. Your money is a prisoner and it is up to people like me to find escape routes for it.

"First rule is that if you have money that is tax-paid capital outside of North America, you can always find a buyer for it inside the capital prison. That buyer will pay you a minimum premium of 10 percent for your free cash. So, a dollar outside North America is worth $1.10 here. There are many instances that give rise to these circumstances.

"There are also opportunities that come up to move your current pools of domestic capital, such as retained earnings or RRSP money, corporate retained earnings, or capital gains into your offshore structure. There are even financial and professional vehicles for moving money out of the country."

"Why all the effort, David?"

"It has become necessary because the government has

placed all sorts of reporting rules on the movement of capital. So, although you may have a structure, you could have problems funding it. If you try to wire transfer funds out, the government wants a record. You can't send cheques because that would connect you to the structure. That has become their way of fighting the offshore.

"What I have to do is find ways that will provide a paper trail for CRA to see where your money went. That paper trail has to be legitimate."

"The other feature is I charge full commission. I don't feel that this is an imposition for the client because these accounts do so little trading that it would be hard to make a living off them. It seems everyone who gets into tax avoidance soon recognizes that because their risk profile is lower, they don't have to take high risks to achieve very comfortable returns."

"I've never understood that thoroughly. Could you explain that to me?" I asked.

"Sure, but it will cost you a beer and I have to pick up my briefcase first. It's in the lounge."

As we climbed the stairs, I began to wonder about my education in tax avoidance. It seemed that the tuition fees came out of a barrel. The more I learned, the more beer I bought, and the more often I visited the urinal. At the current rate, I would either have to learn somewhat faster or kiss my liver goodbye. When we reached the top of the stairs, David told me he wanted a draft beer so I ordered a pitcher to save myself further effort as I could see I was in postgraduate school, which required heavier tuition.

He pulled a folder out of his briefcase, which was sitting on the floor in front of the doubles court. From the folder, he pulled out this diagram.

"As you see," he said, "on the bottom line, I have shown the level of reward and on the vertical axis, the risk generated by that reward. If you are a taxpayer and you want to

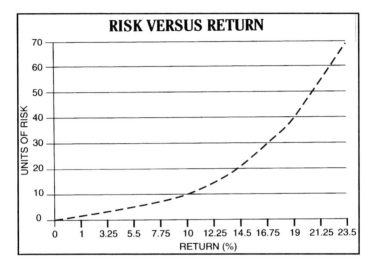

achieve an 8 percent rate of return, what gross amount would you have to earn?"

"At current tax rates, I'd have to earn 16 percent to net 8 percent after tax because I lose half of the earnings to taxation," I said.

"Look what happens to your risk level while moving from an 8 percent to a 16 percent return. Risk triples for a mere double in return. So, when you see the ads for the mutual funds showing a 16 percent annual growth in value, recognize that the net to you is only half of that, and for that you've had to take on a pretty substantial amount of risk.

"My clients' ideas of risk are to buy low-quality bonds

in Canadian dollars and hold them to maturity. If they are not trading, I'm not making any money."

"It certainly sounds fool proof, but I'm still having difficulty visualizing the structure."

As he reached into his briefcase with a flourish, David replied. "Voilà! A flow chart."

THE CORPORATE STRUCTURE

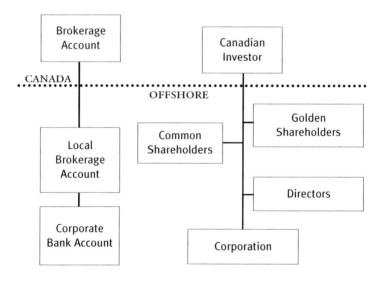

As I looked at the flow chart, it all began to make sense. There was a line dividing Canada from the offshore. Obviously the brokerage account and the investor remained in Canada while common shares of the new company rested with a management company in the offshore jurisdiction. I noticed that David had shown his structure with the B shares being held in trust for the individual in the foreign location.

"Why do you have the preferred shares held outside of Canada, and who is it that holds them?" I asked.

"For the terminally paranoid, I have shown the Golden Shareholder to be outside of the country because of the fear that the holder may get sued and the share show up in his asset base.

"Leaving the B, or golden share, in the foreign jurisdiction is not a necessity of the structure. The possession of the common shares by the management company is very definitely a requirement as that relieves you of any ownership or control responsibilities of the company.

"The fund's flow follows the chart. The money starts its journey in Canada, changes ownership in the foreign jurisdiction, and returns to Canada."

"It does seem quite simple," I said. "But it doesn't show how the vehicle is controlled."

"I could have shown that by drawing a dashed line that went from the investor to the corporate bank or stock account. It is in that way that investment decisions become actions. However, you'll notice that I have shown the bank account as a dashed line. Unless there is a very good reason to have the bank account, I recommend against it. I'm sure you know that the banks now want disclosure of the beneficial owner. If a bank does not want that information, you have to be skeptical because all major established banks now seek that information. If they don't, I would doubt the security of the bank and most definitely insure my funds."

"This structure appears ironclad," I said. "I can see why you are so enamoured with Angelo. He has made you a success."

"It's not all gravy," he replied. "The smart brokers are opening offices right in the tax havens. Take a look at some of the Canadian banks* and brokers. They are in every tax haven in the Caribbean. They are getting to be serious competitors because they take the order directly from the bank in the tax haven and no information regarding the account shows up here. The disadvantage is that your securities might end up in some backwater."

"It seems to me that you are placing a lot of faith in the local broker," I said.

"Those local brokers, in most instances, have been set up as a convenience for the offshore customer. But, if you are still concerned about their integrity, you can go to one of the misnamed North American private banking operations attached to the major banks."

"Ah," I said, "that's what is meant by those discreet little mentions I hear in banking circles. But why do you call it a misnomer?"

"Private banking really refers to a bank in which there is no public stock. The capital of the bank is provided by the partners. A real private bank is one such as Bordier or Mirbaud in Geneva. There are few private banks in North America. I've never been able to see any advantage in dealing with a private bank and the private banking offered in Canada is just a discreet service provided by the publicly listed banks."

"What do you mean by 'discreet service'?" I asked.

"It's hard to know, Stew, but I believe that the commercial banks are starting to muscle into the tax-driven business that is being offered by people like myself. You see, I have

---

*CIBC has indentified the tax havens as a growth area and bought First Caribbean International Bank. You can now bank with the Canadian Imperial Bank of Commerce in the Bahamas and everywhere else.

over $120 million under administration just in offshore corporate accounts and that amount is doubling every two years. It is the fastest growing financial business in the country. What bank can afford to overlook it? The other private brokerages are also seriously into the offshore arena. One of my competitors, who will remain unnamed, has a vice president in charge of the area of offshore investing."

"Aren't they worried about exposure?"

"What exposure? I, with my accounts for offshore corporations, am doing nothing illegal. Suppose my accounts were for Sony, Fiat, and British Airways. Would that change anything? I don't know or care who their shareholders are and it doesn't matter."

"But there is a difference." I said. "Your accounts are avoiding taxes."

"If Sony, Fiat, and British Airways are working in the best interest of their shareholders, then they are avoiding as much tax as possible also."

"If everything is legal, then why all this secrecy and confidentiality?" I asked.

"To begin with," he said, "the system does not use secrecy to avoid taxes. The avoidance results from the structure. The secrecy is there to maintain the system in place. The taxpayer is at war with the tax collector. They are fighting, as is the case with all wars, over assets. In this case, the asset is money. Now, if you are at war and you develop a secret weapon that is winning the day for you, are you going to brag to your opponent that you are using it and how it works? The first thing the enemy would do, under those circumstances, is find a counter measure for your weapon. You would then have to go to the trouble of developing a new secret weapon."

"I think the war analogy is taking things a bit far," I said.

"Not really, the war has already claimed its first casualties, Stew."

"You're stretching my credulity," I said.

"You obviously haven't heard of the Debora Stephan case.* The Stephans were presented with a tax bill for $27,170 by CRA. They couldn't afford to hire an accountant to verify the amount, so they capitulated and tried to negotiate a payment schedule. But CRA, while acknowledging in case logs that the family of twelve was trying to live on $767 a month, applied pressure on the Stephans to pay up, claiming that their budget calculations were 'highly unrealistic.'

"On January 30, 1994, Debora Stephan killed herself. Her suicide note directed her husband, Tony, to use her life insurance payout to cover their tax debt. Years later, when Tony Stephan obtained the CRA ACSES diaries, and discovered 'fairness guidelines,' he launched a lawsuit against CRA for wrongful conduct leading to his wife's death."

"Wow! That must have caused some rethinking at the tax office," I exclaimed.

"It's hard to say. What I do know is, that same year they audited a company started by Linda Stephan, his daughter. I don't know whether it was connected, but the timing was interesting. The problem with that attack was that the company was less than a year old and had yet to file a tax return."

"I don't understand. How can you audit a tax return that hasn't been filed yet?"

* See *Tackling the Taxman.*

"Stew, I said you are at war. And if CRA's audit of Linda was indeed a response to Tony's lawsuit, perhaps they thought the best defence is offence. Attack at dawn even if it looks stupid.

"I look at it, Stew, as if I'm in the trenches fighting for the economic survival of the country. Most of the money that I invest for the offshore client is invested in domestic corporations. It provides the capital for them to expand and create wealth and jobs. If that money were to go to the government instead, the only thing that would expand would be the lifestyle of the politicians and their friends. There is no question that the country benefits vastly as more money flows into its capital markets. Look at Hong Kong. As a result of its flat, 17 percent tax, the country has been a steamroller in growth compared to our puny backhoe. Instead of putting their earnings in the pockets of politicians, the Hong Kongers put it into investments. I'm helping this country by increasing the size of its capital markets. Who is losing out from my activities? The politicians. They can no longer bribe blocs of voters with my clients' money, and they will attack anything or anyone denying them that capability."

I once again found myself bound for the washroom. My bladder was about to burst as I had been entranced by David's zeal and his system and had neglected to interrupt him. As I stood there, I thought about what David had said about taxation and a country's progress. I remembered that the Romans had destroyed the financial centre on the island of Rhodes by imposing a tax there and opening a tax-free port on the island of Delos. However, my real concern was that when I left the club, I would have to go home and have dinner with my wife's obnoxious cousin, Wayne, and his equally repulsive wife, Sheila. I walked back to say goodbye to David who was engrossed in the doubles game being played in the court below him.

"I have to leave, David. I have an obligatory dinner to attend."

"I'm sure that we'll talk again," he said. "You'll want to have the best weapons available in your ongoing battle. I think my armaments are better than anything else in the field. You might as well join the victors in the battle for financial survival."

Here David was talking about winning and all I wanted to do was survive. However, my real test of survival was going to be putting up with Wayne for three or four hours. Once a year, at Martha's insistence, we had her cousin and his wife over for a solitary dinner. We didn't invite any other guests as this would have been an unfair imposition on them.

I always referred to Wayne and Sheila Bell as the "labels." This title arose from the fact that Wayne in particular had to have branded products. The Gucci label had to be prominently displayed on his tie. Instead of his initials on his custom-made shirt, he had Turnbull and Assers. When the gas-station attendant cleaned the windshield of his Mercedes, he always insisted that the model designation on the trunk be shined as well. He once remarked to me that people would not be able to tell I had an expensive watch because it didn't have its brand name prominently displayed. I couldn't make him understand that it was the watch I wanted, not brand recognition.

CHAPTER 8

Wayne's
TAX WORLD

I wanted to describe to Martha all that I had learned from David at the squash club this afternoon and was in the process of doing so when the door bell rang. It was, indeed, cousin Wayne about 15 minutes early with his lovely wife whatever her name was. You could never tell because of all the labels she wore. I'm sure if she was ever struck by a car, the police wouldn't be able to determine if she was Liz Claiborne or Gloria Vanderbilt from the labels sewn into her clothes.

Wayne was an entrepreneur involved in importing and marketing any sort of product anywhere in the world. I guess this explained his love of brand names as he was constantly involved with labelled products. At present, he was involved in a major business of buying jeans in Turkey, attaching Levi's labels to them, and selling them throughout the Middle East as the genuine product. Although I don't usually get into a game of one-upmanship, I was going to hit him with the tax avoidance thing. Knowing him, he probably was unaware of what the clever people were doing.

"What would you like to drink?" I asked.

"A glass of Haig Pinch would be nice," Wayne replied.

"That's Scotch, isn't it?"

"Yeah. It's the best Scotch there is," he said.

I wasn't going to shatter his dream with a discussion of all the other Scotch whiskeys that were possibly better because it would involve labels he didn't know. As I handed him a glass of Johnny Walker, he asked, "What have you been up to? It seems like years since we've talked."

"Oh, I've been looking into the offshore as a possible vehicle for tax avoidance."

"So, you're finally making the move, Stew. I always thought you paid too much tax but I didn't want to say anything. I should set you up with my accountant. He has done wonders for me."

I couldn't believe it! Cousin Wayne was into offshore tax strategies. I was certain he was bluffing. He never spoke of investments or the market. It had to be smoke and mirrors. I decided to play along.

"What has your accountant done for you?" I asked.

"You take the blue jeans business. Boy, did he do wonders with that one. What he did was he set up a subsidiary company of my Canadian company in the Barbados."

Oh great, I thought. He has gone and set up an offshore deal in a country with a tax treaty with Canada. The boys in Ottawa know his every move. "How did that help?" I asked.

"The blue jeans are bought in Turkey by the Barbados company, which then labels and packages them. They are marked up in price and sold to Greece, Israel, and Spain. The offshore company then pays 2.5 percent tax on the income in Barbados and returns the profit to my Canadian company tax free."

"You realize," I said, "that CRA knows everything you're doing because there is a tax treaty between Canada and the Barbados."

"Of course, that's the joy of it. Once the tax has been paid in Barbados at low rates, the remaining profit is considered 'exempt surplus' and returned to Canada without tax. It is then considered as tax paid for Canadian purposes."

I had seen the use of the offshore for transfer pricing. My introduction to that came when I was looking into the financing of a stock-exchange listed company that wanted an injection of capital. The company's business was retailing clothing. While doing my due diligence, I found that 60 percent of the company's purchases came from one company in the Caribbean. I was surprised by this because I did not know of a major clothing manufacturing industry in the West Indies.

What I found was that the Caribbean company purchased clothing from all over the world, marked up the price, and then sold it to the public company. This then went on to explain the low level of profitability of the public company as most of the profit was taken in by the Caribbean company. I suspected that the offshore company was owned by the principals of the public company who kept the profits for themselves. In any case, we didn't do the financing because the shareholders were being ripped off.

Because of this other clothing company's tax-avoidance strategy, I was curious why Wayne chose to pay any tax at all.

"Wayne, why don't you use something like the Cayman Islands and pay no tax at all? You could have an offshore company, buy the fake Levis, and sell them without any reporting in Canada."

"Not smart, Stew. You see, I need the money in the business. If I do the deal in the Caymans, then when I repatriate the money, I have to pay tax on it at full rates. As it is, I pay 2.5 percent to the Barbadian government and nothing to Canada, but I have the use of the money here. I could get myself into a real tax mess with a non-treaty country when I tried to get hold of the money. It would probably be taxed at full rates.

"But why the sudden interest in this? Are you getting into the trading business?"

"No, I'm looking at it from the investment point of view. Sort of like setting up private mutual funds for North Americans in tax-free countries."

"Oh yeah," Wayne said, "I heard about that. Some guys in the Caribbean have designed a set-up where they start a mutual fund under some special circumstances and the investor gets the capital gains tax free."

Oh Christ, I groaned inwardly, not again. He was being even more specific than I was. Here I was talking about the standard offshore corporate structures and he was referring to a brand new system being devised in the Caymans that used the mutual fund regulations to give the investor an offshore tax-free ride. It was so new that even Angelo hadn't heard of it and David hadn't mentioned it. I wasn't going to expose my ignorance to him so I changed the subject.

"Wayne, another Scotch?" I asked.

"Sure. The same."

"That was Haig Pinch, wasn't it?"

"Yeah. Always the best," he replied.

This time I brought him a Teachers to see if there would be any recognition of the change. I might as well have taken a blind man to a strip bar.

"This offshore thing is going to be big," he said. "Is that little bucket shop of yours getting into the business?"

"No, Wayne. Our little bucket shop, as you call it, is the biggest volume dealer on the exchange and we do so by dealing with only institutional clients. We have no retail accounts. I was looking into the offshore," and here I stopped myself and changed my response, "for a friend."

At this point, the ladies arrived from the kitchen. Sheila, Wayne's wife, was drinking a glass of white wine that in her mind was a Mersault as that was the label on the bottle but I knew it was an Australian Chardonnay relabelled for her discerning taste. The Chardonnay was probably a better tasting wine than the Mersault in any case. "What are you boys talking about?" she inquired.

"Stew was telling me about his interest in the offshore and I was telling him how we had been using it for years."

"Oh yes," said Martha, "Stew and I have come to the realization that if we don't start putting some money away offshore we could end up destitute. You know there probably isn't going to be much left in the way of government health care or pensions when we get old. I guess you could say — it's lifeboat time."

"Actually," I said, "I was telling Wayne that my primary interest in the offshore was for a friend."

I could see the light of recognition go on in Martha's eyes. She knew that with her cousin's tendency to portray himself as worldly, anything we might tell him would soon show up in the living rooms of other label worshippers throughout the continent. As Angelo had pointed out, we were our own worst enemy when it came to financial secrecy. To help Martha out of the bind she was in, I said, "Martha and I have been looking at some offshore investments in other currencies and markets to protect ourselves from a fall in the currency." I could see relief spread over Martha's face as she fell into step with my redefinition of the offshore.

"I've been thinking about the Caymans ever since you mentioned setting up there, Stew. You know, that has some merit. I don't have to bring all the offshore money home. I could split off some of the business and run it through a Cayman company and not repatriate the profits. It would all be tax-free earnings."

"It is not quite as simple as you make it out to be, Wayne. Because, if you are currently doing business with a customer base and product line that you are importing to the Barbados and supplying to North America and you suddenly switch that line to a tax haven and supply the same customers, the tax boys are not going to accept it. You should use the transfer pricing method with a new product or new markets."

"Of course, Stew. Everybody knows that. As I understand it, if I bring the product into a tax-free zone and then add some value, such as packaging or manufacturing, then I can mark up the price in the tax haven and sell it. I was thinking of having the labels for some fake Izod shirts, which come from Turkey, sewn on in the West Indies."

I always marvelled how a man with such lack of sophis-
tication and the taste of cretin could be so erudite in
business. He was right. If you added value to a product as
it passed through a tax haven, then there was no problem
in marking up the price.

If you could show that the offshore company was an
active business, then even if you owned 100 percent, it
would not be treated as part of your personal income
stream. To be active, it had to have five full-time
employees. I guess if you were re-labelling fake blue jeans
or Izod shirts you could have a full-time work force. However, unlike cousin Wayne, I didn't have the luxury of
providing fake labels to the masses and any company I set
up would be for investment purposes only and considered
passive and its earnings my personal tax liability.

"Listen Stew, if your research into the offshore comes
up with something cute, give me a call."

"What do you consider 'cute'?" I asked.

"Now don't go blabbing this around, but my accountant
figures that my Barbados company can set up a trust in the
Turks and Caicos Islands for us and it would be tax free.
You see, Stew, if the settlor of a trust isn't a Canadian and
the beneficiaries are, then CRA can't tax the trust as a Canadian entity. He says the Barbadian company isn't a
Canadian resident. That's what I consider cute."

Good old Wayne didn't have it completely worked out
but he had the basic idea of a format that was just being
developed as tax avoidance for Canadians. Wayne's flaw
was that he didn't realize that the company setting up the
trust could not be controlled by a Canadian, but I was
ready to scream. Here I had been working my butt off for
a week gathering information and this fold-out from a

men's fashion magazine had all the state of the art informa-tion. "Where did you pick up all this information?" I enquired.

"Stewart, you've got to get around more. You hang out in those stodgy bars with all those stock market jocks. They know how to make money but not how to hold on to it. I spend my time with the trend setters who know how to make it and keep it. Tax avoidance is the thing today. All the really en courant people are into it, big time. Nobody in my crowd believes in the government fairy tale."

My concern wasn't so much that Wayne had managed to one-up me on the tax avoidance subject, but that it was becoming so common. There were bound to be repercus-sions. I decided to get rid of Wayne by refusing his request for yet another Courvosier Cognac. "I don't think it's a good idea for me to give you another drink, Wayne. I wouldn't want you and Sheila to bang up that beautiful Mercedes."

"Stew, don't worry about it. I'm trading it in for the new model with the garage door opener gizmo built into the dash."

"You don't have an electric garage door, Wayne."

"I know, but with this new car I'll have to get one."

As Wayne and Sheila were leaving after what I consid-ered an overextended visit, I said to Wayne, "Nice Rolex. How do you know it isn't a fake?"

"It doesn't matter," he replied. "If I don't know, then nobody else does either. It looks like a Rolex, and that's what counts."

"Yeah," I said, "that's how I feel about my Dauphne Odjig painting."

"Oh, is it fake? I always thought it was real."

"Good night, Wayne."

Wayne had the ability to leave me completely exhausted in the space of three hours, but his effect on Martha was even more debilitating because she tended to turn off her hearing when he was rattling on. This evening she had wanted to hear it all but had missed some of the fine points. "Stewart, is what he's doing legal?"

"It certainly is, my sweet. What he has done is set up an active company in a very low tax jurisdiction that has a tax treaty with our country. Once tax on the earnings has been paid in the offshore company he can repatriate the earnings to his local company as tax paid. Actually it is not that original. The former Prime Minister Paul Martin took advantage of that Barbadian deal for his offshore shipping empire."

"Why can't we do something like that?" she asked.

"To begin with the tax rules which were changed in 1991 allow only offshore companies or IBC's (International Business Corporations) in international shipping to earn their money tax free even if controlled by a resident Canadian. When it was found that some Canadians might have to pay income tax on the capital gains incurred from their shipping activities the tax laws were further changed retroactively to make capital gains from shipping non-taxable. The only people who can have tax free offshore income are those in international shipping such as Paul Martin. Hell, the Department of Finance even had the St. Lawrence River and the Great Lakes proclaimed international waters for tax purposes. Unless we start an international shipping line like Canada Steamships we will have to be content with trying to set up an active company in the Barbados.

"The critical word is 'active.' His offshore company is a

real-live functioning entity with at least five full-time employees and the whole enchilada. In Wayne's case it supplies a service and enhances the value of the product, even if it is only sewing fake labels on fake jeans. Our offshore company would not be considered active by the tax man and as such we would not be able to shield its earnings."

"The other thing I don't understand, Stew, is why the federal government allows people to set up businesses in foreign areas with low taxes and thus avoid domestic taxes?"

"It's to provide economic stimuli to some of the poor countries."

"If low taxes stimulate economic activity abroad, why can't that be used to stimulate our own economically depressed areas?"

"Here, at home, the pork-barrel factor rules supreme. Although lowering taxes may be the more efficient way to stimulate job creation as opposed to the system of grants, which do you think would sound better to the masses: 'Folks, I just arranged a reduction of corporate tax rates for new businesses established in our riding by 50 percent to lure new employers to our community.' Or, 'I just arranged an $84 million tax-free loan to the local airplane company so they can keep on working.' In this latter case, you are appealing to the local union bosses and suppliers. In the first case, the new plants might be non-unionized, use different suppliers, and put pressure on the deadbeats in our society to take work. That may be acceptable in foreign dominions but we can't have that sort of radicalism here, and to make things worse, it won't guarantee our politicians' re-elections."

"The other thing that is bothering me," she said, "is

that he makes it sound like everybody in town is now into tax avoidance. If they are, then government revenues are going to start to fall and the tax collectors are going to get more vicious. I would feel happier if you checked with a lawyer before we went too much further on this."

"Firstly, my dear, bear in mind that if Wayne is into something then he believes that it is the new wave and the great wave. That is not always so. However, you are right about the legal advice. I was thinking that myself. I'm going to call on the best in the business."

CHAPTER 9

Torts for LUNCH

We met at La Fenice on King Street near John where the chef was cooking up a spaghettini with clam sauce for me and an agnolotti for Larry, our corporate tax lawyer. I had offered to buy Larry lunch if he would look at the tax planning I was considering. He was our corporate lawyer because he was the only one we could find who could give us a legal opinion on one sheet of paper. He was, therefore, brilliant.

"When you called and said it was something personal, I told you, Stew, I don't do that kind of law."

"I know. But this is different. I talked to one of my ex-partners and he described a system of tax avoidance to me that sounds simple but effective." I then went on to describe to our corporate lawyer the system Angelo had described to me.

"I've gone to a bunch of lawyers and all I get is gobbledegook. You know — 'on the one hand this and on the other that' and 'notwithstanding this but agreeing to that,' which of course tells me nothing. You know how to cut through all the crap. Tell me, will this work?"

"Yes, from what you have told me, the strategy you have described would work and you are breaking no laws. If you went to the IRS or CRA, they would say don't do it. They wouldn't want you to even try. To discourage you, they would quote the anti-avoidance laws irrespective of their flimsy legal basis. However, if you did it and at some point in time the tax authorities found out that you had followed this route, they might ask you to unwind it and they might even ask for back taxes. The question hinges on their finding out that firstly, the company exists only to defer your tax liability to some date in the future and secondly, the amount of tax that has been deferred. It would seem to me that the taxation people would say that you have avoided, not evaded taxes. At no point, did you lie to them. Every action you have taken is quite legal. You can incorporate a company. You can manage the investments of any other legal entity. You can be the signing officer on a bank account of which you are not the beneficiary.

"Your problem would hinge on the question of what was your intent. This is what CRA describes as 'mind and management.' Obviously, if your intent was to avoid paying taxes on the investment earnings at this time, then that is tax avoidance. That is not a crime but it does run afoul of CRA's anti-avoidance rules, which state that although tax avoidance is legal, they don't like it. Under those rules, it seems that the worst they could do is force you to unwind the deal."

"I've heard that new structures have been designed to overcome the reporting requirements."

"That's true. So, what have the tax sleuths got as a result of someone having the special shares of a foreign company? The amount, from what you tell me, is less than 10 percent of the class, so that person doesn't have a foreign affiliate," he replied. "That certainly isn't illegal. Neither is your signing authority on a foreign bank account. The corporation would certainly have no reporting requirements to anyone.

"The only connection between you and the tax-avoiding structure is your telephone. Obviously, at times you may call the bank in the Turks if you go that route, but from what you tell me, you will be following a conservative investment stance that won't require constant communications between you and the bank. If you are dealing with a foreign stockbroker for the company, you might be advised to have a personal account there as well to justify the phone calls. If you choose to use the system outlined by your friend, David, you will be calling a broker in the Turks so if you are worried about the calls to the islands, open an account personally with a few bucks in it. But that is getting pretty paranoid. Remember, you are only required to report all your worldwide income, not your assets."

"I wouldn't let that be a concern," I said. "My buddy tells me that the financial engineers have already designed a corporate structure to overcome that problem."

"Well then, as I see the circumstances, it is not your income and you don't report it. The taxers can ask about your sources of income but they can't come around snooping at your phone records without getting themselves into trouble. They can't ask you personal questions other than the most personal — what amount of money did you earn. Questions as to whom you phone or what you own are none of their business. If they insist on asking you these types of questions, my recommendation is to hire a real scrappy lawyer and phone an investigative journalist. With the current mood in the country, there are a number of writers who would love to do a piece on the illegal activities of the tax department."

"But what about when I start taking the money out? There will be a direct link to me," I said.

"Of course there will, but you will be reporting the income as dividends, consulting fees, or a retainer from a foreign corporation and be paying tax on the funds received. All of which is quite legal."

"Supposing they ask where or how the company earns the money it pays me?"

"Then you direct them to the company's offices and have them ask the company. Remember, you are not an officer or director of the company and you can't know. You are an investor."

"But, the company won't tell them anything," I said.

"Well, it seems there is a standoff. You see, Stew, it is not enough to know that someone is avoiding taxes; it has to be proven. If you have no records of the activities of the offshore corporation in your home or office, how is anyone going to come up with a number for the amount of avoided taxes? As well as looking at the principle, you must also look at the practical aspects.

"The most likely cause of an investigation into your tax avoidance practice will probably arise with you. At some moment, you may indiscreetly brag about your ironclad pension or whatever you want to call it, and someone who hears this may, in a fit of envy, take it straight to the tax department. Also, there is nothing like a disgruntled spouse as a source of information in the eyes of the tax investigators. Incensed wives have been known to report all of their husbands' records to the government in spite of the fact that doing so will diminish the size of the pot to be distributed between separating spouses."

"Give me the one page summary," I said.

"Here it is. The government will not want you to do this because it is a tax-deferral scheme and they want money now. They cannot stop you from doing this. If you ask them for an opinion, they will turn your scheme down under something related to section 245 of the *Income Tax Act*, the general anti-avoidance rules. If you ask them and do it anyway, you will certainly be in trouble. If you don't ask and do it and they can find some way to look into it, they may ask you to unravel it and pay back taxes. From a practical point of view, I can't see how this could ever be found out and to what extent amounts could be determined. Even if it was found out, you wouldn't go to jail."

"Why would they ask me to unravel the set-up if it is legal?" I asked.

"Because you are winning the battle for the tax dollar. I am not sure if you know this but you are not supposed to win. It's like Las Vegas. If the casino owners see a constantly winning customer, they throw him out."

At this point, Adreano, the waiter, brought the bill. I had reached for it when Larry covered it with his hand and said, "Tell me how to get in touch with the guy who set this up for you and lunch is on me."

CHAPTER 10

The Expense
ACCOUNT WARS

. . . .

That night I drove home much more content with my understanding of the offshore situation than I had been. Larry had reassured me that everything I was doing was legal. I was sure that Martha would be as mollified as I was. When I arrived, I was happy to note that little had changed in my family life while I was out gathering information. Duncan was surfing the Internet looking for sleaze or weirdness and Katherine was spouting some conventional wisdom she had heard in a women's study group. To expand Katherine's consciousness, I asked her why men outlived women in Bangladesh but not in North America and could the reasons be juxtaposed. To get Duncan away from the information highway's answer to *Playboy*, I had him find out in that vast library of his why the Jews rebelled against the Romans in AD 66 and fled to Masada. Having sidetracked my children from tawdry pursuits, I went in to report my most recent findings to the love of my life.

"I spoke with Larry the lawyer at lunch."

"Where did you go?" she asked, "La Fenice?"

"I had to. You know how Larry likes good Italian food and anyway he picked up the tab."

"Well, that's a first. What did you do — promise him a judgeship?"

"He was so happy to learn about tax avoidance that he paid for lunch."

"You could have really made his day by sending him to my cousin, Wayne," she said. "As well as becoming en courant regarding tax avoidance, Wayne might have given him a deal on some fake Levis. Tell me, what did Larry have to say?"

"As far as Larry can see, we are not committing any illegal acts by following the system Angelo outlined. He looked at each event in the chain and determined its legality and found that none of them violated existing laws. Also, he pointed out that we are not denying the government their piece of the tax pie, we are just delaying when we pay the tax. It's a tax-deferral plan.

"I thought about it on the way home. It is no different than a registered retirement plan or a 401-K plan in the U.S., except that it can't be seized by creditors or the government. Also, there are no limits as to how much you contribute or what type of securities we buy. We could have the whole thing in Swiss Franc bonds if we wanted to."

"That's fine, Stew, but you've now hit another road

block. How do we get the money? Suppose there is a medical emergency and I have to take you out of the country for care. How do we get hold of the money?"

Well, this was something I hadn't thought about. I had been so engrossed with the idea of getting money into the damned thing that I clean forgot about getting paid back. It was great to have a million bucks stashed somewhere but how do I get it back?

"Angelo is coming for dinner tomorrow," I said. "I'll get a bottle of Amarone and a Cohiba cigar and if you'll do that fine ossobuco, we should be able to get him talking."

I arrived home the following day to the smells of wonderful Italian cooking. The kids were still trying to find answers to the questions I had asked them the previous day, so all was well in the household. Martha had gone out of her way to prepare a great meal. All I had to do was the dessert, which was a chestnut vermicelli with whipped cream. I always mix rum with the chestnut purée. I've got Martha convinced that it is necessary to dilute the purée and rum is the only acceptable liquid. As I was whipping things up, Martha asked, "What are we going to do about your uncle Harry?"

"What do you mean? He's not coming over from England, is he?"

"No, Stewart, I mean about the solicitor's letter and the will."

"Oh, I'm sorry, my dear, I hadn't told you. I've got Paul working on a trust with the English lawyers. They are setting up a trust in the Caribbean with the funds at Barclays Bank. Although the trust is registered in the islands, it will be administered out of England. I wanted to discuss with you what you wanted to do about the payments. How to take them and when. You've got survivor rights if we are still married when I die, but what about the kids? At this time, it seems that Duncan's only interest is his computer monitor and Katherine seems to be suffering from middle-class guilt.

"I can't think of giving out a lot of money to those two offspring of ours. They seem to be complete air heads."

"You may be a bit harsh, but your general thoughts are right. Leave it with me and I'll do some research on how to handle Harry's legacy in the best interest for us, our children, and if things work out, our grandchildren. I only wonder how far out of the grave you want to reach?"

"Aside from that, my dear, bear in mind that whatever our children receive will be taxed to death because of past government wastefulness. If we leave them anything, it has to be in a tax-efficient manner."

"Not necessarily, Stew. The whole system is breaking down. When people, such as my cousin, Wayne, whose every thought is generated by some twit at a fashion magazine, is starting to talk tax avoidance, the collapse is nigh. In the words of Bob Dylan, 'The times they are a-changin.' We can't know what the tax system will be in ten years time."

"Therein lies the problem, Martha. Trusts tend to be inflexible. Maybe Angelo will have some answers."

At this point, Katherine came into the kitchen looking quite pleased with herself. "I found the answer, Daddy," she said. "Bangladeshi women have shorter lives than their husbands because they work themselves to death supporting their husbands and families. Isn't that cruel? How did you know that? I didn't know they had feminist classes when you went to school, daddy."

"Katy, you've done a great job answering half the question. What about the second part, which is why do North American men die before their mates?" I inquired. "Is the answer the same?"

At this point, Martha, ever the good mother, tried to spare her daughter further embarrassment.

"Sweetheart," she said, "can't you see that Daddy is just toying with you? Why don't you just forget the question."

After Kate had left the kitchen, I said, "Martha, she's never going to learn reality if you just keep deflecting her from fact." It looked like we were going to get into a good debate as to when children had to be weaned from their fantasies when the doorbell rang.

Angelo arrived with "the lovely Sarah" as he called his wife. She was clutching a beautiful bouquet, and he a bottle of Brunello.

"We always have fresh-cut flowers on our boat, Stew," Sarah said. "It's a pleasure everyone should enjoy."

"Well, don't enjoy this too soon," said Angelo. "This wine needs at least another four years in the bottle. Sort of like a good deep discount bond. You get the pay-off at the end."

Angelo looked great in spite of the fact that I had heard that he had come back here for surgery. After the pleasantries, I asked him about his medical problems. "Did you come back for a penile implant?" I asked jokingly. The pain I felt from Martha's elbow in my ribs was, however, no laughing matter.

"I'm certainly in no need of that," he guffawed. "No, Stew, I made some mistakes a few years back and I am now paying the price.

"Two years ago I was playing tennis in Florida and I tore my Achilles tendon. It's quite a common injury in males over 50."

"Well, that hardly counts as a mistake," I said.

"No, my mistake was in leaving Florida and coming to Toronto for medical care. As you know, I can take my medical care anywhere in the world with my private health insurance. However, the Orthopedic and Arthritic Hospital had my old medical file and did some great work on me when I ruptured the cartilage in my right knee some 20 years ago. So, I figured why not go back to the shop that did the best job. Big mistake. The hospital wasn't the same as it was 20 years ago when the governments were lavishing borrowed money on the medical system.

"Sarah called them late in the week and described my injury and asked to set up an appointment. Apparently things are so bad there, that an injury as severe as a torn tendon has to wait until their clinic is open on Wednesdays.

"I went to their clinic and a young fellow named Marks examined my leg. He accepted the diagnosis of a torn Achilles tendon. Sarah asked him what were the available courses of treatment. He replied that there were two options — one being a plaster cast and the other being surgery. Sarah asked what was the best course of treatment, to which he replied surgery. She asked me if I was willing, and when I agreed she told him to get going on it. He left the examining room and came back a few minutes later saying that maybe it was better if we put a cast on the injury instead.

"Sarah caught on immediately and asked if his change of treatment was brought about by the lack of operating space. The good doctor admitted that they didn't have an operating room available. When Sarah asked if we could wait until space was available, he told her it would be too late for surgery. This was, of course, after another of their doctors had told Sarah that time was not critical and made me wait five days for an examination. The end result is that the improperly treated leg is starting to cause me problems in my knees and hips. I'm going in for a major surgical procedure to try to repair it. If they had done it at the start, the costs would have been about half the $10,000 it will now cost."

"Why come back if the care is so bad?" I inquired.

"There are still some good practitioners here in Canada. They are leftovers from the old days when money was poured into the health system. If you can find one of these guys and offer them cash, you can get pretty good work. Remember, their earnings from the provincial coffers are capped. Money from outside the provincial health-care system is worth more than standard earnings. The only caveat is that you have to set everything up in advance."

"You have universal health insurance, why not get the surgery in the U.S.?" I asked.

"We thought about that. You know they are terribly efficient down there. I understand that they run their high-priced equipment, like MRI machines, 24 hours a day, unlike here where they close down after the day shift and let them stand idle. But, there is a ringer. The price of medical care is the same in Canada as in the U.S. But, if you buy it here in Canada, you pay with 85-cent dollars, so you get a 15 percent discount. I figured, why not save the insurance company some money and keep the premiums down.

"But, you know, Stew, it is kind of crazy. I can come here as a non-resident and buy health care but you as a resident can't buy it here. You have to leave Canada to buy your health care. So, if you end up with a heart condition and they tell that you have to wait six months before you can get it fixed, you have no other options but to go outside the country.

"But what about you, Stew? Are you still grinding along in the old firm?"

"I am," I said, "but I keep hearing more stories like yours and I am getting worried. I think the government pension is a dud as well. So, Martha and I are looking for a lifeboat. We figure that if we don't take steps now to protect our future, it could be pretty bleak. As a result, we are looking into the offshore. My conversation with you as to how to set things up was very helpful, but once I get to that point, I don't know what to do."

"My concern, Angelo," said Martha, "is that once we get the money into the offshore we won't be able to get it back."

As we devoured a wonderful veal shank, Angelo went over the fine points.

"Let's assume," he said, "that you've parked some money in an offshore structure for 20 years and you've continued to top it up. It would in all likelihood be worth about a minimum of a million dollars.

"How much were you thinking of starting with?" Angelo asked.

"We thought we would sell our mutual-fund portfolio and move the 200,000 into an offshore corporation," Martha said.

"In that case, you are more likely to have well over a million dollars in 20 years."

"That raises two questions, Ang," Martha remarked. "The first is how much money do we bring back each year? The second, how do we account for the earnings?"

"You only bring back what you need. If you and Stew are living quietly during the first few years, you won't need much. However, should you decide to take an around-the-world cruise, then you would have to bring back more.

"As for how to account for the money, you would use a common format employed by industry and government. You would become a consultant to the offshore corporation and receive a retainer. The government does it all the time. High-level bureaucrats and members who have lost their seats are taken on as consultants to a government bureau with loosely defined responsibilities and big expense accounts. Often, part of the kickback to corporate managers and directors who facilitate a friendly takeover of their firm is a consulting contract."

"Angelo, I have never understood why they do that," Martha said.

"It's a tax efficient way of getting money into the individual's hands and it sounds better than a kickback. If you were to give the person involved a big one-time payout, most of it would be taxed at the high marginal tax rate. If you spread it out as smaller amounts over a period of years, the net amount of after-tax dollars in the recipient's hands increases. However, the big bonus in those situations is the expense account. Take your situation. Martha and you may want to go to Vienna and attend the Opera Ball some winter. If you timed a business trip to Vienna as the consultant for the offshore corporation, you don't have to pay income tax on the price of the trip. You get a 50 percent discount. That's better than any frequent-flier program I've ever seen."

"Isn't that an abuse of the system?" Martha asked.

"No. If you want to see real abuse of the system, take a look at your elected representatives and their expense accounts. In Canada, they are given very substantial tax-free expense allowances to accommodate their costs of having to go back and forth to their constituencies and maintain two households. So far so good. The abuse is that rather than spend that money for those ends, they gave themselves credit cards and free airplane tickets a year to cover those costs.

"Do you think it was people like me that came up with these methods of getting the tax-free bucks? No, you just look at what is going on in government and industry and bring it down to the individual level. Think about it. When the government postulated new rules for offshore reporting to stop tax-avoidance abuse, did they mention expense accounts? They wouldn't dare because any legislative bills that would have to go through Parliament that included a shutdown of the expense-account abuses would never get passed by the members using that system of tax-free income generation. If a bill limiting expense account abuse ever got past Parliament, it would never get through the senate. In Canada, senators are given a tax-free expense allowance, free unlimited first-class travel for themselves, children, mistresses et al., and the ability to charge up to a further $50,000 in expenses to us taxpayers without receipts. Therefore, be thankful to your representative's greed that the expense account remains the best way to enjoy your savings tax free."

"It still doesn't seem right," I said. "Didn't a member of the Canadian government named Blondin recently get punished for misuse of her government credit card?"

"No, Stewart, Ms. Blondin was not punished for the misuse of her credit card. When it was discovered that she had bought a fur coat with her card, her explanation was that she considered it a legitimate expense because she was showing solidarity with some of her constituents who were fur trappers. Like so many phony expense-account expenditures, justification requires creativity. But, I am sure that you can see that her excuse stretched the boundaries of credulity. It was, therefore, not accepted and she had to give the money back. Had she been in the corporate world she would have been fired, but just because those nosy reporters happened to expose what was being perpetrated throughout Parliament Hill, government leaders felt there was no reason to single her out. But look what that decision has done to the reporters who went to the trouble of finding the abuse. No real punishment was dispensed so it is unlikely they'll bother following up on that line of investigative reporting again.

"The same is true of the tax department. They, first off, would have to become aware that you took that trip to Vienna and then determine if it was in fact business rather than pleasure. That's a lot of work for a lousy couple of thousand bucks in taxes. To be able to hound you, the tax sleuths would have to get all the charges on your corporate credit card and ponder the legitimacy of each. The only ones that would be cut and dried would be purchases of goods and even that gets debatable. Why did you purchase that antique English partners desk for ten grand? To do the company's work on, of course. If you were ever to sell such an article, you would surely return the money to the corporation. After all, it is the property of the corporation."

"I hear what you are saying, Angelo. Treat the expense account from the offshore company the same as you would any employer's business credit card and only use it for expenditures you could justify as business."

"It is being done every day. Thousands of people are

using their expense accounts on the very boundary of personal versus corporate expense. When it becomes too flagrant, as happened in Vancouver, where a multi-millionaire was using the corporate jet to go on vacations in the Caribbean and to get to the opera in New York, the taxers will come along and deem the expenses personal and demand income tax on the value received. You just have to use discretion.

"There are two other considerations," he said. "The first is that you don't want to be using the credit card until you are in some way employed by the offshore corporation. Otherwise, the question might be asked, 'Why are they paying your expenses?' So, when you come to the point where you are living off your foreign income, make it legitimate by earning a consulting fee from the corporation rather than a salary. If you take a salary, then the expenses might be deemed a taxable benefit arising from employment. Hell, you never know. By that time, the government may allow the rest of us to have the same tax-free $26,000 they give themselves in expense money.

"The second point is that you should use a credit card with a bank that does not make your credit-card records available to third parties. If someone wants to see your records, then they should have to ask you for them directly rather than the current North American practice of going behind your back. Remember, you don't want to evade taxes by using the credit card, but you want to make your business travel coincide with your personal needs. If someone wants to challenge your credit-card charges, then they should have to deal with you directly. Most foreign banks, such as the Standard, Standard & Chartered, and Barclays, will not expose your offshore bank records to our local authorities and that includes your bank-card billings. But it has to be an offshore bank. Domestic banks are completely beholden to the taxers.

"Seeing as we are talking about income," Angelo said, "you would have to show any cash you received on your tax form. Of course, you would pay tax on it as any law abiding citizen would. If you didn't, that would be tax evasion. If you are considering tax evasion, I would suggest that you first run for high public office."

"I don't understand that part, Angelo. What do you mean by 'high public office'?" I asked.

"It seems, Stew, that tax evasion is not a crime if you are in the government. It occurred that the Clintons, when Bill was governor of Arkansas in 1980, made $10,000 in trading profits but neglected to mention it on their 1980 tax form. When the press brought the matter to light in 1994, when Bill was president of the U.S., he and Hillary paid the tax on the outstanding amount and the interest but they didn't pay any penalties. Nor were they charged with tax evasion. Here in Canada the head of the Mint took over $400,000 in expenses in one year."

"I hear you," I said. "I can't think of any politician in North America being charged with tax evasion. I guess they are all straight arrows."

"Yes, and the tooth fairy wears green bowling shoes. So avoid any trouble and just pay your taxes," Angelo said.

"Why would we go to all the expense and trouble to set up an offshore business and account," asked Martha, "if we are just going to end up paying taxes anyway?"

"If you get the ownership of the income-producing asset out of your hands, then the income will grow tax free as in your pension plan. In the end, the amount available to you will be greater. However, when you start to receive income, you have to pay tax on it, albeit at a lower rate as you will have no employment income, being retired."

"Hold on a minute everybody," I said. "You are all making a big assumption. That being that we will be dipping into our offshore nest egg while being resident in North America. We could just as easily be taking the proceeds in Ireland or Costa Rica where there is no tax on offshore income," I said.

"Stew's got a good point. We don't know what your circumstances, or the world for that matter, will look like in 20 years. If the countries continue to fragment into smaller components, people may regain control of their governments and the tax and spending policies would end, leading to lower tax rates. Or, we could see the collapse of income tax either through ineffectiveness or a revolt, which I would say is what we are discussing at this moment. In that case, the world would move to consumption taxes in the form of value-added levies. One thing you can be sure of is that the Laffer curve will dictate that higher income taxes would be self-defeating. Therefore, it is unlikely that in the years to come your income will be taxed as heavily as it is now."

"One feature I like about the offshore is the independence it provides," I said. "You know, it is not out of the question that North Americans may be required to collect our local pensions here rather than abroad. The governments could impose even higher withholding taxes to stop people from collecting their North American pensions outside the continent. As well, I read recently that one of the hot new ideas to top up social security was to put a one-time charge of 15 percent on all pension-plan assets held outside of social security. It now seems that taxes and rules regarding pension plans can be put in place after the fact. With our nest egg offshore, it would be safe from any such hare-brained schemes.

"Tell me, Angelo, why not just take out the earnings as dividends on the preferred shares?" I asked.

"There is nothing to stop you receiving dividend payments from the offshore corporation to finance your retirement. However, remember that you will not be entitled to a dividend tax credit as you would with Canadian dividends or any other special tax treatment that depends on your residency, because the dividends are from a foreign corporation and, hence, treated as ordinary income by the tax department. Also, you would not be able to have that one great asset, the expense account. You could, however, accommodate that problem by taking a combination of both dividend and consulting income," he said.

"Angelo, if you were in our shoes how would you do it?" I enquired.

"In your case, Stew, you should have the company appoint you as a consultant. You would then take a retainer with possible bonuses should your cash need an increase."

"Wouldn't that look fishy?" I asked.

"Why? There are many individuals on retainer to the government or to an industry who do nothing and receive a stipend. Can you find any reason that the tax department would harass them if they are paying taxes on those stipends? Also, if you are on retainer, you might be able to take some non-cash benefits, such as travel or the use of assets like cars and lodging. However, here is where some discretion is warranted.

"The nearer the benefits that you are taking approach cash, the more watchful the tax department will become. Supposing you had a credit card issued to the corporation and were using it for personal needs. In some situations, the tax department would penalize the card owner, which in this case is a corporation, and disallow the expense for tax purposes.

"However, the corporation that owns your card is not resident in Canada and can't be punished by CRA. The tax guys would then come after you. They would say that the payments made by the corporation on your behalf are, in reality, the equivalent of cash and, therefore, earnings."

"You're kidding," I said. "Politicians in Canada and other countries have been getting exactly that, a tax-free spending allowance, and it isn't called income for tax purposes. Hell, in most cases they don't even spend it. They bank it."

"Stew, the politicians in all countries have different rules for themselves than they do for their constituents. But, let's look at another potential benefit. How about travel? You realize that the offshore corporation may want you to go to Mexico in the dead of winter to examine the potential for doing business there. It may be such a complex situation that you and Martha would have to go every winter, all expenses paid of course.

"Then there is that monetary conference at the Davos ski resort in Switzerland every late winter. The offshore corporation may want you and Martha to attend that to find out what the economic future might look like. We can't stop the politicians from doing exactly that and it is just as hard for them to stop you."

"Now you stop that!" Martha said with a big grin on her

face. "We might begin to feel as guilty as the local politician does as his nose gets even deeper into the trough."

"Martha, don't mock. It gets even better," Angelo replied. "How would you like to have a nice red Porsche 911 parked in the driveway? You wouldn't own it of course. It would be owned by that friendly offshore corporation. Mind you, the keys would be in your purse."

"I'm beginning to like the sounds of this," Martha replied. "What's the downside with the car?"

"Because the tax department wanted to reduce the value of tax-free goodies that corporations gave their employees, they limited the amount of the taxpayers' tax-free car allowance. They did this by putting a limit on the value of the car you could provide to an employee. Over a certain value, the cost of the car is no longer deductible for tax purposes by a corporate taxpayer. In your case, the off-shore company couldn't care less because it has no income against which it is going to take deductions in Canada. If you wanted, they would provide you with a Rolls-Royce."

"How far can you take this?" I asked.

"We really don't know the limits yet. There are jet planes, yachts, and residences owned by governments and industries all over the world. They are reserved for the use of some privileged individuals at no cost to them. Why not join the club?"

"What if we don't live long enough to spend it all?" Martha asked.

"You win again," Angelo replied. "Your heirs will get the remnant money without any taxes being withheld. If they were to inherit the money from within Canada or the U.S., they would lose a portion of it to the tax man."

"That could be an even greater threat in the future,"

Angelo's wife said. "You know, the governments are running out of room in the income tax field, so asset taxes will have to be increased."

"Angelo, you haven't explained how we pass on the offshore money to the children when we die," Martha stated.

"While you are both alive, I expect that you will both be signing officers on the offshore company's bank or stock accounts. Then, if either of you dies, the system continues for the survivor. If you both die, the children would probably hold the special shares that would give them control of the company."

"The special shares are bearer shares and whoever possesses them owns them. Your survivors could then demand that the remaining funds be paid out to them in the form of dividends if they wanted. My advice to your children would be to have the offshore-company administrators set up new situations for them so that the money never comes back to North America."

"But, what about the inheritance tax on the special shares?" Martha asked.

"There is none," Angelo said. "If you die in Canada, the government will tax your estate on the basis of its capital appreciation. The special shares will not have appreciated, being worth exactly what they were at issue, which is nominal. If you die in the U.S., the shares will certainly fall below the constantly shifting ceiling of tax-free allowance for inheritance and you will own few other assets."

Being a corporate organizer, I could see some difficulties looming. "Angelo, how can the administrators send cheques to the kids if both Martha and I are dead? The administrators don't have signing authority at the bank."

"With ownership of the special shares, your kids could ask the administrators to change the signing officers at the bank or brokerage. With the advice of the administrators or someone like myself, they could soon set up a system that is most beneficial to themselves.

"But you know, Stew, the combinations and permutations you can use with trust law and corporate law open a whole smorgasbord of possibilities of structures to accommodate heirs. A couple of very wealthy individuals who consulted me decided not to have their offshore money go directly to their children or grandchildren. In the articles of incorporation, they have left instructions that upon their demise, the assets of the corporation will be placed in a trust. Seeing as neither the settlor, which is a foreign corporation, nor the controller of the trust is Canadian, it is not taxable in Canada and the heirs are left with untaxed income. The benefactors, as well, come away with the comfort of knowing that their heirs can't blow the bundle."

"I heard that in 2000 the budget changed the viability of Trusts. Aren't they crippled?"

"There was some very draconian and some very funny law proposed by the Finance Department in 2000. The draconian was, when you cut through all the verbiage, that if a dollar originated in Canada it was Canadian no matter where it resided and would be taxed as Canadian. It was quickly pointed out such legislation would trap some of the governments most loyal fans such as people with offshore shipping empires that originated in Canada and trusts that were in the midst of moving billionaire's funds out of this country tax free.

"The funny part was that the feds said they were going to tax foreign trusts that might have Canadian beneficiaries. Brilliant! The trust says it's not gong to pay Canadian tax and Canada can't collect. I can't think of what air head thought that one up. Needless to say, when saner minds thought of the consequences and applications of the 2000 tax reforms they cried in their martinis. They tried to revise it in 2003 only to be told that the whole thing was too dangerous to the source of funds for the Liberal Party and impossible to apply."

"Ang, it's very comforting to know that you have all this wealth offshore just waiting for you, but what happens if you need cash for an emergency?" Martha asked.

"What sort of emergency do you mean?"

"Well, suppose Stew was diagnosed with a brain tumor. You may not know it, but those things are very time sensitive and I would want Stew to be scanned by the latest technology now, not at some future date established by the government hospital's waiting list."

"That is an interesting question. We are allowed to have private schools and police forces running in parallel with the government's systems, but not health care, so you could not buy the health care you wanted in Canada. But, you could buy it in the U.S., and I know just the offshore company that would be willing to lend you the money to take a trip to the Mayo Clinic and cover all the diagnostic expenses. Once having been diagnosed, you could then return to Canada and demand the appropriate response. If it is not forthcoming, then another foreign venue might be sought for the operation. You could have it done anywhere in the world."

"Of course," I said, "there is nothing to stop me from borrowing from anyone, including a foreign corporation. In the situation Martha described, a bank would never loan you the money because there is the possibility that the borrower might die. Also, I could never get the money out of my pension plan without taking a terrible tax penalty. But, if I borrowed from the offshore corporation, the money would be here overnight and if I were to die, the loan would be paid out of my estate back to the lender, thus preserving Martha's tax-deferred nest egg. You know, Ang, this is beginning to sound like an insurance policy."

"Stewart, uncertainty creates risk. Smart people insure against risk. As we grow older, we can't be sure of what genetic land mines have been laid in our path. After age 40, your health starts to get to be an uncertainty. You have to insure against that risk. The North American democracies are financially impaired and unable or unwilling to fulfill the promises made in the heat of election. Impaired governments do stupid things — how can they not? Remember, it was a financially impaired Germany that brought you Nazism."

"Ang, if Martha and I want to pursue this insurance, is there an agent here?"

"There is a fellow here, in Toronto, representing a company from the Turks and Caicos, who will either look after your needs or steer you to someone who can. He is a zealot on this subject and has helped hundreds of people prepare for their retirement with safety."

"He operates legally in Canada?" I asked.

"Of course his operation is legal. I often see his ad in the national newspaper in the business classified section under the heading 'Offshore Services' and he is in the phonebook.

"If you are thinking of using one of the vendors of offshore companies, be sure to ask if they have consulting capability to ensure that your structure works. Many individuals and companies operating in this field only want to sell a corporate shell and have very little knowledge of how these are used. Remember, you don't want the company to be a foreign affiliate and you do want the ability to get money into the company."

My digestion improved dramatically. I kept thinking in terms of an insurance policy. This was really my whole reason for looking into the offshore and it now looked like my research was done and implementation was the next step.

CHAPTER 11

Haven a
REAL GOOD TIME

Our dinner the previous evening with Angelo had been very informative and I now felt I had all the tools necessary to establish an offshore situation. I was, however, surprised to get a call from our neighbour and tax lawyer,

"What's up?" I enquired.

"You know that your wife hired me to look into the future inheritance from your uncle Harry. I've been speaking to his English solicitors and I think that your situation is as tax benign as possible."

"How benign is that?" I asked.

"No tax."

"Don't say anymore. We shouldn't be talking about this on the phone. You never know who's listening."

"Stewart, ease up. This is all terribly legal and if you want, you can run it by the tax boys, although I wouldn't. Once you become known to them, they never let go of you. I need some information from you, so let's get on with it — the meter's running you know."

"Okay, what do you want to know?"

"When do you want to retire?" he asked.

"In 15 years," I said.

"How do you want the money in the trust managed?"

"Have it invested in index funds in U.S. dollars."

"What are index funds, Stewart?"

I explained to our lawyer that index funds were structured to reflect the composition of the market generally. I chose the Standard & Poors 500 as my index. My reasoning was that as an investment professional, I had seldom seen a fund manager consistently outperform the stock market on a continuing basis. Therefore, rather than pay for active management, I was content with just having my money grow in line with the stock market. My costs would be lower and I would never underperform the market. No surprises, either good or bad.

"Let me ask some questions," I said. "First off, what is happening with my possible legacy?"

"I've spoken to the English solicitors and they want to set up a Bahamian trust regardless of the fact that I wanted Turks and Caicos as the residency. Because they work for Uncle Harry, it seems that they will get their way as to where the trust holding your inheritance is going to reside."

"What are the features of the Bahamian trust?" I asked.

"The trust will be set up in the Bahamas for a period of 15 years after which time it will be dissolved and, if you want, reformed. It also has the following nice features.

"The first is that it will be governed by the 'Fraudulent Dispositions Act of 1991,' which will require anyone wanting to unwind the trust to prove, within two years of the trust's formation, in a Bahamian court, that the assets were deposited to avoid existing creditors. What that does is get rid of frivolous attempts to break the trust. Therefore, after two years you can rest assured that the trust is safe and secure. Anyone trying to overturn Uncle Harry's will, will be forced to do it quickly and then apply to the Bahamian courts. It looks to me that once the inheritance is there, it will stay there.

"The second feature is that the Bahamians have implemented laws that will not allow a judgement obtained outside their country to be used to attach assets in a Bahamian trust. A judgement has to be obtained in a local court to pursue assets in a trust.

"The third feature is an anti-duress provision. If you are forced by a court order outside of the Bahamas to require the trustees to do something that will diminish or jeopardize the trust in any way, the trustees have the ability to disobey the request and re-establish the trust in another jurisdiction, such as the Turks."

"What about confidentiality?" I asked.

"It's covered by the Bahamian 'Confidentiality Act of 1965,' which prohibits banks, trust companies, and their employees from divulging information about customers or accounts. There are financial and jail penalties for violation of the act. The secrecy is impeccable. But why are you worried about secrecy? This is completely legal."

"It may be completely legal today but, as in the revolutions in China and Russia, it may become a crime to own wealth at some time in the future. You know that the sanctity of private property is not enshrined in the Canadian Charter of Rights and Freedoms, and the Americans are even worse off with their seizures of property under the guise of crime or terror fighting. It's pretty difficult for someone to steal something from me if they don't know I have it."

"You're right, Stew," Paul said. "I think I'll take that attitude in all my tax avoidance and asset-protection work. Confidentiality leads to security."

"You've always advocated the Turks and Caicos Islands to me as the location for offshore trusts and corporations. Why did the English lawyers choose the Bahamas?" I asked.

"The Brits felt more comfortable dealing in the Bahamas, probably out of familiarity. They agreed with me that virtually all the features of the Bahamian trust were available in the Turks, but in their typical British fashion, they informed me, 'We always do business in the Bahamas.' There was nothing I could do. I think it might end up costing Uncle Harry's estate more to set up in the Bahamas than in the Turks. However, they assured me that, with the rules I mentioned to you governing trusts and the fact that there is no financial or fiscal information sharing between the Bahamas government or any other, your nest egg would be safe.

"The other reason for my call is to ask you how you want the trust to look after Duncan and Katy."

"Martha and I talked about that. We decided that if Harry dies while either one or both of the children are in university, then the trust should pay the equivalent of a year's tuition at Yale to each of the children while they are in school. Once they finish the undergraduate level, they are on their own and would receive nothing from the trust until five years after both of us are dead and then they are to split the proceeds."

"That sounds sensible. Is there anything else?"

"Yes. Very importantly, we want the right to be able to borrow from the trust."

"That shouldn't be a problem," Paul said.

"What about costs? Is the trust going to cost me anything?"

"Not a dime, Stew. There are no income, personal-asset, or withholding taxes in the Bahamas and the trust's maintenance costs of about $2,500 a year are borne by the trust. You have absolutely no worries about your Uncle Harry's trust. That said, how about a squash game tomorrow? Can you get a court this late for Saturday?"

"I can't tomorrow, Paul. I've got an appointment with a consultant to talk about setting up offshore."

Saturday morning I had to give up my leisurely sojourn in bed, during which I usually read the weekend paper, and instead, I popped out of bed as if it was an ordinary work day. It was a pleasure driving to town without the usual crush of traffic. I found Liberty's office, which was located in a downtown apartment block. Upon arrival, the fellow introduced himself as Lex. He apologized for dragging me into town on a Saturday but he said that his work week would be full for the next couple of weeks. I asked if there was a rush to set up offshore.

"No. It's just that the government has brought in this '$100,000 rule' and the 'Foreign Affiliate rule,' so I'm busy with corporate reorganizations for my earlier clients so that their offshore companies are no longer foreign affiliates. Also, as a result of the corporate reorganizations, the value of their holdings has to be rolled back to $99,900. I feel obliged to do this for free although I'm not the one who caused the problem. Even though I'm not charging a fee for this work, my clients are still having to fork out about $250 per corporation to change the structures.

"Some clients are choosing to roll their offshore assets into a trust to avoid the continuously changing Income Tax Act. So, if I have ruined your weekend, Stewart, blame it on Ottawa's bureaucrats."

"I am very intrigued by something you just said. As I understand it, there is a corporate structure that allows an individual to hold an offshore company without it being considered a foreign affiliate."

"To be more correct, there are a number of ways of organizing the foreign company so that it does not become a foreign affiliate."

Lex went on to describe the alternatives to me. They were variations on financing methods currently being used by my own corporate finance department every day! It was all so simple.

"How much is this going to cost me?" I asked.

"It'll cost you $2,000 to set up and $2,000 per year to maintain. I do mean dollars not dollarettes."

"What are 'dollarettes'?" I asked.

"They are dollars, such as the Canadian and Hong Kong dollars, which have not yet grown up to have the purchasing power of the U.S. dollar," he replied.

"So we're talking U.S. dollars. That 2,000, does it include the first year's fees?" I asked.

"It does, Stewart. But, now it is my turn to ask some questions. Where do you want to establish this company?"

"The Turks and Caicos Islands," I said.

"Do you and your wife want to be signing officers on the corporate bank or stock account in the Turks?"

"Yes, that way we will be able to move the money from the islands by just writing a cheque. Also, if either of us dies, the survivor will have access to the money."

"Do you want a bank account for the company outside of its jurisdiction?"

"Yes, I want an account in Douglas, the Isle of Man, with both my wife and I as signing officers on the account."

Lex described to me an optional asset-management company that would handle all of the details of the investments with the added benefit of keeping the securities in either Canada or Europe with a brokerage account in which assets could only flow in, or if they were allowed to come out they would go to a location I chose. He said it would be easier than dealing with a bank manager in the islands.

I left an hour later with two forms in my pocket and a commitment to come back on Monday with a photocopy of my passport as well as Martha's. The passport copies were used to verify our signatures and existence to the bank authorities. They would go no further than the bank. I only had to get bank letters of reference for myself and Martha. The documents I carried were signature specimen cards for Martha to sign. Our only tie to the entire structure was our bank documents.

When I arrived home, Duncan stopped me at the door. "I found the answer to the massacre of the Jews by the Romans in AD 66." Although I already knew, I decided to play along.

"What was it?" I asked. "Religious persecution? Political independence?"

"It was taxes. Can you imagine that? As far back as the birth of Christ, there were tax rebellions. The Jews were required to pay a tax to the Romans as well as their own temple. After the first tax rebellion and the theft of the gold from the temple, the Romans sent Titus to negotiate a peace in Judea. Titus offered the people peace if they would accept Roman hegemony (which was already a fact) and if they promised to pay their taxes. They refused on the latter point and rallied under the Zealots to fight the Romans. They lost and fled to Masada, a natural fortress, and harassed the Roman tax collectors. The Romans would probably have left them alone if they had not interfered with the tax collectors. The Romans finally managed to breach the defences but found that the occupants had committed suicide.

"It appears, Dad, that their timing was bad too. It seems the Romans experienced ongoing tax revolts and crushed each one with increasing force. They made an example of the Hebrews, which then provided a respite from tax revolts."

"What did you conclude from your research?" I asked.

"That taxes and tax revolts have been part of the human fabric since time began."

"While you're thinking of tax revolts," I said, "correlate that to the Laffer curve."

"What's that, Dad?"

"Why don't you do some research and tell me?"

At this point, Martha came to the hallway and when Duncan had left, asked me why I continued to prompt him into doing research that was irrelevant.

I explained that our children were being bombarded with propaganda that closed their minds rather than expanding them. Unless they knew the realities of life, they would be exploited.

"I don't want them to grow up blindly believing every politician and Messiah that walks their way."

"It's just a phase. They'll get over it."

"Don't believe that," I said. "Your government has poured millions of dollars into groups continuing to promote fake fears and consequences to deflect the population from considering the realities of their leaders' profligacy and incompetence. However, if you accept that the children can't handle the truth, then here is a truth they cannot know until we are on our death beds. I spent some time with the offshore provider and we are on our way to moving our savings out of the country. I don't want you to tell anyone what we've done; although it is legal, it takes control of our assets out of the hands of government and they hate that. Also, you never know what restrictions they will impose in the future.

"We should tell the kids about Uncle Harry's inheritance ending up in a trust because they may get some benefits of the trust if he dies before they finish university."

"What about the asset-protection trust we discussed?" Martha asked.

"I've thought about it but it doesn't really work for us now. The asset-protection trust works best with liquid assets and by the time we move our savings offshore, there will only be the house to protect because all of our liquid assets will be out of the country."

"Stewart, we got started on this endeavour mostly to protect our assets and now you are telling me that we are going to leave the house exposed to those vultures proposing to sue your partnership?"

It was at this point that I again realized what an emotional issue the house or nest is to women. I could see that Martha was really upset. "Look," I said, "so far this guy is only threatening to sue. But, if it will make you feel more comfortable, what I will do is set up a domestic corporation to buy the house and sell the shares to the offshore corporation. It'll mean that I have to file an annual income tax form every year for the company owning the house but that shouldn't pose a problem. To set up the local corporation, it'll cost about $1,200, and it will probably cost the same in land transfer fees but at least we won't have any assets if someone takes a run at us. That's cheap insurance," I said.

I could see the look of relief spread over her face. That calm presided over the dinner table while Duncan explained to us the implications of the Laffer curve. I went to bed that night feeling very relaxed. However, when I went to sleep my recurring nightmare started. It involved a holiday that Martha and I took in the Caribbean. In the dream, I'm swimming in choppy water when all of a sudden a shark appears and starts to chase me. The face on the shark looks exactly like a tax auditor I encountered six years ago. Usually, I wake up just as the shark reaches my legs. This time, I swam to a place where the water suddenly turned calm. I looked behind me and the shark had stopped at the boundary of the smooth water and the choppy seas. He remained in the chop. At this point, a black man rowed over in a boat and offered me a rum punch.

"Not now," I said. "You've got to help me out of the water or the shark will get me."

"Relax, mon," he replied. "He can't get you here. You are in the shark-free zone. They can't come in here." I woke up just as I reached for the rum punch.

ABOUT THE AUTHOR

Alex Doulis was born in Vancouver in 1939 and graduated from the University of British Columbia.

He worked for a number of years as a geologist in Alaska and the Yukon. He was also employed in Utah and Ontario as a mathematician in the early days of computers. His field of endeavour was the application of computers to the analysis of financial problems. He took this experience to the investment industry, where he toiled for 19 years.

While on Bay Street, he was one of the highest-ranked analysts in his field, a partner at Gordon Securities, and a director of McNeil Mantha.

He has spent the past fifteen years living tax free on his yacht in the Mediterranean writing and travelling.

You may contact the author at his website www.alexdoulis.com.